Fifteen Years
Of Fear

Fifteen Years Of Fear

An Introductory History To
The Opening Chapter Of
America's Cold War Story

Jared D. Williams

Copyright © 2018 by Jared D. Williams.

Library of Congress Control Number:		2018914195
ISBN:	Hardcover	978-1-9845-6950-9
	Softcover	978-1-9845-6949-3
	eBook	978-1-9845-6948-6

All rights reserved. No part of this book may be reproduced or transmitted in any form or by any means, electronic or mechanical, including photocopying, recording, or by any information storage and retrieval system, without permission in writing from the copyright owner.

The views expressed in this work are solely those of the author and do not necessarily reflect the views of the publisher, and the publisher hereby disclaims any responsibility for them.

Any people depicted in stock imagery provided by Getty Images are models, and such images are being used for illustrative purposes only. Certain stock imagery © Getty Images.

Print information available on the last page.

Rev. date: 11/30/2018

To order additional copies of this book, contact:
Xlibris
1-888-795-4274
www.Xlibris.com
Orders@Xlibris.com
788466

Introduction

The era between the year 1945 and 1960 should be viewed as the opening act to one of the most frightening productions of historical theater ever recorded. Over this fifteen year span, fear gripped the world as the two remaining superpowers positioned for global dominance. Divided by support for one side or other, the modern world found itself relying on allies, and distrusting potential foes more firmly than ever before. One of the world powers held a deep desire to rule the world while the other superpower threw its money, resources, and the lives of its young men into the effort to thwart the other's ambition. The world had emerged from a world war that sought to end the ambitions of tyrants and dictators only to become frozen in another struggle. That struggle proved the sad reality that ambitious nations like the Soviet Union could still rise in the political climate of the mid-20th century.

During those years, atomic bombs were tested only to become obsolete and replaced by even deadlier and more destructive weapons. Both nations became capable of delivering payloads of death to millions around the world in just a matter of minutes. Bomb shelters were built in an attempt to ease the minds of those who were caught in the potential path of the seemingly inevitable destruction. Fear caused by the anxiety related to the potential end of the world hung over the heads of the citizens of both sides. The Cold War had firmly placed the world in its terrifying grip and would not free mankind for decades.

Those first fifteen years of the Cold War set the stage for the remainder of the rivalry between the United States and the Soviet Union. Thankfully, the era proved that inevitable wars do not always come to fruition. This is the story of the United States and American leaders who shaped the nation during those first fifteen years of the Cold War. Colossal men with larger-than-life legends dominated the era with names became synonymous with the period. Truman, MacArthur, Eisenhower, Nixon, Kennedy, McCarthy, Kennan, and many more rose to the occasion, or fell victim to, the Cold War's paranoia. Either way, their story, and the story of the collective United States, is one worth telling.

This opening era of the Cold War can be condensed into the Truman years and the Eisenhower Years and is often told by the men who served under them. Both men firmly planted their legacy on the Cold War, but did so through varying approaches. Even though Truman ordered the dropping of the first (and what would be the only throughout the Cold War - due in part to his and Eisenhower's leadership) atomic bombs in the history of warfare, some of his policy decisions gave the appearance that he was stuck in a mindset belonging to an era before the Cold War. This mindset would bring about the "limited war" of Korea. Eisenhower on the other hand, quickly and accurately realized the nature of war was forever altered at Hiroshima and Nagasaki.

Truman was a reluctant president who done the best he could do and rose above expectations. Still, Truman needed Eisenhower as a trusted general until the collapse of the friendship blossomed into a political rivalry. Eisenhower was ready to assume the mantle of the presidency from a lifetime of preparation as a student and active participant of the U.S. government, military hierarchy, international affairs, and handling emergencies with global implications.

Two men who would later shape America's Cold War strategy came of age during this era. John F. Kennedy and Richard M. Nixon both entered the Washington limelight and quickly rose up the ranks of their political parties. Both served in World War II and like all men of their generation, they had their worldviews shaped by the events surrounding America's rise to a global power. They were often friends, destined to be rivals, linked through their attachments to Senator Joseph McCarthy, and journeyed together on their destiny to become firmly cemented in 20th Century

American history. But make no mistake, this era helped create the Kennedy and Nixon of the history books that we know today.

Domestic issues took on global importance during the era as America struggled to keep their message of spreading freedom from being damaged by the stain of segregation and the horrors that too often attempted to squash the Civil Rights Movement. Dr. Martin Luther King, Jr. would spend time in jail, African-Americans were beaten by police, and the violent images of their struggle went out around the world to the delight of the Soviet leaders. America had to find ways to spread the freedom at home they wanted to be the champion of around the world.

This era witnessed America making the tragic decisions that would ultimately lead to the nation's involvement in the Vietnam War. The United States would leave, officially enter, leave again, and lay the foundation for another entry into Asian ground wars during this time. Many men would give their lives for the containment of communism and dutifully heed their nation's call to arms in the advancement of liberty.

Most people remember the post-World War II era as peaceful and idyllic. Occasionally, the instability associated with the Civil Rights Movement or other hardships are mentioned in casual conversation about the era, but most thoughts and discussion about the period turn to the bliss of the a time after a global war. The economic prosperity, the seemingly solid household structure, the birth of rock and roll, and the early days of television too often overshadow the era's real struggles. While post-war America was a place of innocence, lurking constantly in the background were the dangers of the growing Cold War. Those who lived it knew it. But just like the Korean War, the Cold War's impact on that particular time has been forgotten by most Americans unfamiliar with the depth of American history.

With all things considered, the first fifteen years of America's Cold War struggle shaped the nation for decades to come. The United States often acted valiantly in its noble cause to stop the spread of communism, but dark secrets also litter the historical landscape. This period was a time when the world, as we know it, could have ended at any moment with a brilliant flash of light and the tragic fallout of horrendous weapons. But, that catastrophic end never happened and the reasons why can be mostly be found in the story of the first fifteen years of the United States of America and the Cold War.

Part I

1945-1949

"If we see Germany is winning we ought to help Russia…If Russia is winning we ought to help Germany…Let them kill as many as possible."
-Harry S. Truman

I

Harry S. Truman: A Reluctant President

History remembers Harry S. Truman as the man who stepped up to deliver the final blows to Nazi Germany and the Empire of Japan during the last days of World War II. He has also been remembered for his no-nonsense and folksy approach to running the executive branch between the years of 1945 and 1953. As a leader who stood up to the growing post-war communist threat, many historians would remark that Truman has few equals in nation's history. With all of this accepted history, it is easy to forget that Harry S. Truman entered the White House as a reluctant president. He had never envisioned himself as the chief executive of the United States when the honor and responsibility was suddenly thrust upon him.

By 1944, the United States of America had been under the executive leadership of President Franklin D. Roosevelt for over a decade. Roosevelt emerged victorious onto the national political landscape in the 1932 presidential election. He had already built a fine political career in state government serving in the New York legislative branch, and as the state's governor before becoming president. He had also been the democrat party's nominee for vice-president in the 1920 failed attempt to beat republican Warren G. Harding. In addition, he also served as assistant secretary of the navy under President Woodrow Wilson. Roosevelt brought a lifetime of political experience to the White House that he combined with the lessons learned from the tragedies of personal illness. His experiences allowed him to connect with the American people on a large scale.

Many Americans had grown up with Roosevelt in the White House. Some citizens had almost forgotten what it was like to live with another president in charge of the executive branch of the national government. His was the only voice Americans were accustomed to hearing on the radio during times of crisis. Roosevelt had led the American people through the worst of times. The Great Depression had the nation in its unrelenting grip as he took the oath of office in March of 1933. Now, he had brought the United States through the perils of a world war with leadership that rivaled that of Abraham Lincoln. Roosevelt approached his election to a fourth term in an almost sainted status. No one had ever served as president of the United States this long, and only a select few had been as successful as Franklin D. Roosevelt. By

1944, the bond between the American people and their president was special and strong.

Franklin D. Roosevelt had given party leaders his blessing to add Harry S. Truman to the 1944 Democrat ticket as the vice-presidential nominee to run with him for his historic fourth term. Truman had not actively or publicly sought the nomination claiming that he had no ambition beyond being a senator from his home state of Missouri.[1] At the Democrat convention, he was genuinely shocked when the announcement was made that he won the party's nomination for vice-president on the second ballot.[2] Even though he was aware his name had been brought up by democrat party leaders as a potential vice-president,[3] Truman was still taken by such surprise that he had to put down the sandwich he was eating to address the delegates in the convention hall after being put on the ballot with Roosevelt in the middle of a world war.[4] Truman delivered one of the shortest convention acceptance speeches in history for a vice-presidential nominee.[5] A man who seemed to possess no ambition toward the presidency was now

---

1 H.W. Brands, *Traitor to his Class: The Privileged Life and Radical Presidency of Franklin Delano Roosevelt* (New York: Doubleday, 2008), 769.
2 Ibid., 770.
3 A.J. Baime, *The Accidental President: Harry S. Truman and the Four Months that Changed the World* (Boston: Houghton Mifflin Harcourt, 2017), 96-98.
4 Ibid.
5 Jean Edward Smith, *FDR* (New York: Random House Trade Paperbacks, 2007), 619.

facing an election to be the next in line as commander-in-chief in a changing and complex world.

Harry Truman was fully aware of the dangers facing the world as he ran alongside Roosevelt on the 1944 Democratic ticket. There were still wars to finish in Europe and the Pacific in addition to the growing complexities in the alliance between the United States and the Soviet Union. With these factors considered, Truman often remarked that he was afraid of the nomination.[6] His fears were understandable due to the fact that it was no secret to anyone in the Roosevelt circle, and to the Democratic Party leadership, that the president's health was failing.[7] It was becoming increasing clear that the man chosen to be Roosevelt's vice-president may be taking over the ship of state much sooner than anyone expected. Winning the vice-presidency potentially meant that Truman would soon become the president of the United States.

Roosevelt's health issues were becoming more visible as the election approached. Truman observed the president's failing condition when he visited the White House in the late summer of 1944. He left the meeting with Roosevelt stating he was concerned about the health of the president.[8] In referencing the deteriorating condition of Roosevelt, Truman told his assistant, "I had no idea

---

6   Jay Winik, *1944:The Year that Changed History* (New York: Simon and Schuster, 2015), 476-477.
7   Smith, *FDR*, 624.
8   Ibid.

he was in such a feeble condition."⁹ The Roosevelt/Truman ticket won the 1944 election, but the chance of Roosevelt finishing his fourth term after the election was appearing to be increasingly unlikely.

The western allies' worst fears became reality when President Franklin D. Roosevelt passed away at 3:35pm on April 12, 1945 in Warm Springs, Georgia.[10] Eleanor Roosevelt informed a stunned Harry S. Truman about the death of her husband.[11] Truman was unable to speak as the ramifications of this news began to overwhelm him.[12] Very few men had ever been placed in the position in which Truman then found himself. World leaders from Winston Churchill to Joseph Stalin were grieved by the loss of President Roosevelt. There was also a measure of concern from Allied leaders as to what the death of Roosevelt would mean during a time of war.[13] Understandably, foreign and domestic leaders asked the question: what kind of leadership would come from the almost unknown Harry S. Truman?

The plain speaking man from Missouri was now the president of the United States and nothing could change that fact. Being the last man to occupy the White House without a college degree,

---

9   Ibid.
10 Winik, *1944*, 527.
11 Brands, *Traitor to his Class*, 816.
12 David McCullough, *Truman* (New York: Simon and Schuster Paperbacks, 1992), 342.
13 Smith, *FDR*, 636.

Truman had many reasons to doubt himself as a world leader. For one, he was taking over the helm of the ship of state during one of the most turbulent times in world history. Second, he was following a colossal figure in Franklin Roosevelt. Harry S. Truman now had to find a way to live up to the ghosts of the executive mansion, end a war with the Axis Powers, and maneuver through the increasingly complex relationship with the Soviet Union. All these decisions now rested solely on his shoulders. As president, he had little time to grieve the loss of the beloved American president.[14] Truman faced all these issues as a man who enjoyed leading from the front. As the sign he placed on his presidential desk stated: "The Buck Stops Here."[15] Truman was now in charge and would meet all these challenges head on.

Eleanor Roosevelt summarized what being president of the United States in 1945 truly meant for Harry S. Truman. When Truman asked Mrs. Roosevelt if there was anything he could do for her upon learning about the death of her husband, she replied, "Is there anything *we* can do for *you*… For you are the one in trouble now."[16] All eyes in the free world now looked to President Truman for leadership, courage, and the ability to make the right decisions at the right time. The newly minted President Truman spoke to a group of reporters during his second day as president

---

14 Winik, *1944*, 529-530.
15 McCollough, *Truman*, 481.
16 Ibid., 342.

of the United States. After having lunch at the Capitol, Truman told the assembled reporters, "Boys, if you ever pray, pray for me now... when they told me yesterday what happened, I felt, I felt like the moon, the stars, and the all the planets had fallen on me."[17]

It is impossible to overstate the seemingly insurmountable mountain of duty that faced Harry S. Truman when he entered the White House in 1945. Obviously, he had the difficult task of the current world situation and the expectations of the free world to navigate through the complicated peace that was coming, but there were other factors at play. Many people felt they had just seen one of the greatest men in the history of the United States (in Roosevelt) replaced by an unworthy successor. These expressions are reasonable in light of Roosevelt's death occurring in such historic times, but these fears followed Truman into the presidency. Truman had to follow the legendary figure who had be summed up by the New York Times in the days after his death by writing, "Men will thank God on their knees a hundred years from now, that Franklin D. Roosevelt was in the White House.[18]

Earlier in 1945, President Roosevelt had met with British Prime Minister Winston Churchill and Soviet leader Joseph Stalin at the Yalta Conference. Decisions made at the conference would have major implications in the coming Cold War. Among

---

17 Ibid., 353.
18 Robert Dallek, *Franklin D. Roosevelt: A Political Life* (New York: Viking, 2017), 620.

other issues hammered out at Yalta, the Soviets had agreed to allow noncommunist officials into the Polish government and officially decided to join the war against Japan.[19] The problems of Yalta became apparent as the war began to grind to halt. It became increasingly clear that the Soviet Union had no desire to uphold the compromises made at the conference. Stalin was determined to hold the territory his army now occupied after the defeat of Hitler. Many critics of the Roosevelt administration believed the president had failed to secure freedom for Eastern Europe in the meeting with Stalin.

Now it was Harry S. Truman's turn to sit face-to-face with Stalin and Churchill at the last conference of the big three allied leaders.[20] Truman would be meeting Churchill and Stalin outside the bombed-out capital of Hitler's Germany. Known as the Potsdam Conference, the meeting was the first time America's war time allies could fully acquaint themselves with the new president. The meeting featured some of the biggest personalities in the world. For Harry S. Truman, the meeting also presented him with another moment of potential self-doubt knowing the chair he occupied at the table was meant for the titanic figure of Franklin D. Roosevelt.

Despite the reservations and concerns, President Truman more

---

19 Eirc Foner, *Give Me Liberty: An American History, Volume II* (New York: W.W. Norton and Company, 2012), 875

20 Ibid.,874.

than held his own at the conference. The first decision made at Potsdam decided who would occupy the role of chairman of the conference. With potential underlying motives, Stalin suggested Truman for the role.[21] Winston Churchill then seconded the motion. Harry S. Truman had come a long way in a short period of time. He was unrecognizable to most Americans just a year before, but now he was the chairman of the most powerful meeting in the world.

On the agenda for Potsdam were some of the most pressing issues of the day. The conference would attempt to settle the questions surrounding the post-war future of the German nation. Stalin had not met the compromise of Yalta by refusing noncommunist members of the Polish government to take their place in the new Polish government. The Polish issue later carried major cold war implications, but it was also a matter that needed addressing at Potsdam. China, Italy, and other problems emerging from World War II needed to be discussed as well.[22] It was clear that decisions made at the conference could potentially save the world from another devastating war. The stakes could not have been higher.

Arguably the most significant event of the Potsdam Conference did not happen in Germany but in the United States. While Truman was attending the conference, he received official word

---

21 Baime, *The Accidental President*, 295.
22 Ibid., 296.

that the atomic bomb had been successfully tested and was ready for use against the Japanese Empire. Not only did this news place Truman on sound footing to deliver the final blow to Japan, it also strengthened his hand at the negotiation table.[23] With the successful completion of the atomic bomb, the United States was now the most powerful military power in history.

The Potsdam Conference made major decisions that would impact the worldwide political landscape for decades to come. Among others, the big three leaders decided to keep the previously determined German zones of occupation and removed all forms of Nazism from Germany.[24] Germany would be the potential flashpoint for any outbreak of war between the United States and the Soviet Union for the duration of the Cold War. Also, the United States issued the Potsdam Declaration during the conference warning the Japanese about the destruction of their empire if they did not surrender and end World War II. President Truman was ready and able to completely destroy the Empire of Japan from the sky.

On August 6, 1945, a U.S. plane named *The Enola Gay* ushered in a new form of warfare by dropping the first atomic bomb in the history of combat on the Japanese city of Hiroshima. The city was left in complete ruin. The world would never be the same after the

---

23 Margaret Truman, *Harry S. Truman* (New York: William Morrow and Company, 1973), 268-281.
24 Baime, *The Accidental President*, 327.

bright flash of light incinerated Hiroshima. Travelling home from the historic Potsdam Conference, President Truman announced the news of the bomb to the world aboard his boat. Truman told the shocked world, "We are now prepared to obliterate more rapidly and completely every productive enterprise the Japanese have above ground in any city… Let there be no mistake; we shall completely destroy Japan's power to make war…If they do not now accept our terms they may expect a rain of ruin from the air, the likes of which has never been seen on this earth."[25]

A few days later, the Japanese city of Nagasaki was destroyed by another atomic bomb. This devastation combined with recent U.S. firebombing of Japanese cities and the entry of the Soviet Union into the war against Japan, brought World War II to a close. But the use of the atomic bomb should not just be viewed as the final chapter of the World War II story. The bombings of Hiroshima and Nagasaki were also a part of the first chapter of the Cold War story then taking shape throughout the world. By using the bomb, President Truman saved American lives by eliminating the need for an invasion of Japan. Also, he brought the war to a close before the Soviets could acquire large pieces of land in Asia saving another division of a defeated enemy nation. Keeping the Soviets out of Japan avoided the confusion and dangers found in post-war Germany.

---

25 Ibid., 340.

President Harry S. Truman had held his own among the most powerful men in the world at the Potsdam Conference. He had also ended the most devastating war in human history. Truman's star, and that of the United States, could not have been any brighter at that moment. Unfortunately for Truman and the world, he would not be entering into a time of prolonged peace following World War II. He would find himself on the front line against an enemy as potentially dangerous as any faced in World War II. President Harry S. Truman would have to guide America through the dangerous world of the Cold War. An old ally was becoming a dangerous potential enemy.

II

The Rising Soviet Threat

Following the successful conclusion of the wars in Europe and Asia, President Harry S. Truman soon found himself dealing with a new series of problems. The United States of America's wartime ally was quickly becoming a peacetime nuisance. Joseph Stalin and the Soviet Union became increasingly rebellious against U.S. post war plans as the smoke cleared from the battlefields of World War II. This uneasy relationship was anything but new. The United States and the Soviet Union already had a somewhat rocky history by the time America entered the Second World War in 1941. And as the war dragged on, Stalin was paranoid the U.S. would make a separate peace with Hitler's Germany[1] leaving his nation alone to face the Nazi onslaught; even though it was the "enemy of my enemy is friend" philosophy that held the U.S./Soviet alliance

---

1   Michael Dobbs, *Six Months in 1945: FDR, Stalin, Churchill, and Truman-From World War to Cold War* (New York: Alfred A. Knopf, 2012), 153.

together. Now without the threat of Nazi Germany to hold the alliance together, cracks in the relationship, based on the two nations' fundamental differences in political ideology and post-war world views, reemerged.

The events of the post-war world surely came as no shock to President Truman. He was acutely aware of the danger Stalin posed to the stability of the world. As a senator before the war, he had went as far as to group Stalin with Hitler as a menace to the world saying, "If we see Germany is winning we ought to help Russia…If Russia is winning we ought to help Germany…Let them kill as many as possible."[2] Truman did acknowledge Hitler as a worse option for continued world leadership than Stalin, but only be the smallest of margins.[3]

The Truman administration decided the best way to deal with the rising communist threat was to simply keep it from spreading. The United States adopted a policy of "containment" to achieve this goal. The United States would leave communism where it already was, but would resist all its future efforts to expand. The belief was based in the idea that the Soviet Union would be unable to sustain a long, drawn out standoff with its capitalist foes and would eventually crumble. Due to the impossible task of keeping up with the industrial might of the United States and

---

2   Brands, *Traitor to his Class*, 594.
3   Ibid.

its free-market allies, the philosophy of containment held to the conviction that the Soviet Union would fail allowing satellite states in Europe to escape from the communist world.[4]

Initially, the Truman administration struggled to find its footing in the arena of growing tension with the Soviet Union. Other than occasionally taking on the Soviets rhetorically, President Truman had done little to stand up to communist expansion in the days following World War II. The United States continued to cling to the hope of peaceful negotiation with the Soviet Union.[5] However, Stalin's continued efforts to grab territory out of the ruins of World War II made a peaceful coexistence between the U.S. and the U.S.S.R. become increasingly unlikely. President Truman had to change the nation's approach and find a new way to effectively deal with the rising communist threat.

---

[4] Bevin Alexander, *MacArthur's War: The Flawed Genius who Challenged the American Political System* (New York: Berkeley Publishing Group, 2013), 4-5.

[5] John Lewis Gaddis, *The United States and the Origins of the Cold War: 1941-1945* (New York: Columbia University Press, 2000), 284.

III

The Birth of Containment

In this time of uncertainty surrounding U.S. foreign policy, the Truman administration searched for clarity in its approach to the Soviet Union. Helping to shine light on the growing tension was an assessment of the situation by American diplomat George F. Kennan.[1] Called upon to bring some clarity to the Soviet situation, Kennan delivered one of the most important documents of the Cold War. Out of this document, the foundation of the U.S. policy of containment would arise.[2]

The birth of containment was on February 22, 1946 when Kennan sent his "long telegram" to State Department officials in the United States outlining how best to deal with the Soviet menace.[3] Kennan worked as a young, and somewhat obscure,

---

1 Ibid.
2 John Lewis Gaddis, *The Cold War: A New History* (New York: Penguin Group, 2005), 29-30.
3 Alexander, *MacArthur's War*, 4-5.

attaché at the American embassy in Moscow. In his five part telegram, he identified the Soviets as a legitimate threat to the United States, as well as to the security of the world.[4] It was from Kennan's recommendations in the "long telegram" that the Truman administration would adopt the policy of stopping communist expansion without trying to eliminate communism overall.[5] War would not necessarily be essential according to Kennan, but rather the United States should commit itself to ensuring the Soviet Union faced continuous failures in attempted expansion until the communist leadership abandoned its current ideology.[6]

Kennan's telegram was the longest ever sent in the history of the State Department.[7] He believed the message contained in the telegram was of the utmost importance and had to be sent via telegram instead of other avenues of communication. Kennan decided it was best to ignore potential security risks that may occur from using a telegram to ensure his message was quickly received. His assessment of the Soviet approach was considered marvelous by State Department officials when it arrived on their desks. The telegram was revered as "a splendid analysis."[8]

---

4   Chris Burkett, ed., *50 Core American Documents: Required Reading for Students, Teachers, and Citizens* (Ashland, Ashbrook Press, 2013), 404-418.
5   Alexander, *MacArthur's War.* 4-5.
6   Gaddis, *The Cold War*, 29.
7   John Lewis Gaddis, *George F. Kennan: An American Life* (New York: Penguin Books, 2011), 218.
8   Ibid.

Outlining the concept of containment, Kennan stated in the telegram, "Soviet power, unlike that of Hitlerite Germany, is neither schematic nor adventuristic. It does not work by fixed plans. It does not take unnecessary risks. Impervious to logic of reason, and it is highly sensitive to logic of force. For this reason it can easily withdraw — and usually does when strong resistance is encountered at any point. Thus, if the adversary has sufficient force and makes clear his readiness to use it, he rarely has to do so. If situations are properly handled there need be no prestige-engaging showdowns."[9]

George F. Kennan's clear analysis of the Soviet mindset, combined with concrete evidence of Stalin tightening his grip on Eastern Europe, allowed Truman to transition from tough talk to serious action. The president was ready to make containment the official American foreign policy in dealing with the Soviet Union.[10] The Truman administration was now on a fixed course of action against the communist threat.[11] The United States was taking another serious step toward international interaction that would come to define the second half of its 20th Century foreign policy.

---

9   Burkett, ed., *50 Core American Documents*, 416.
10 Gaddis, *Origins of the Cold War*, 285.
11 Ibid., 353-355.

IV

Containment in Action: The Truman Doctrine

The early months of 1947 demanded much of President Harry S. Truman and the policy of containment. In February, Great Britain notified the United States of their precarious economic situation forcing them to withdraw from foreign affairs. The British had been assisting the nations of Greece and Turkey in the struggles against armed attempts to replace their existing governments with communist leadership. The post-war financial burdens, combined with additional increasing strains on the British economy, forced Britain to abandon being the primary protector of Greece and Turkey. The British hoped America would step in to assist the nations against communist aggression.[1]

Knowing that Congress would have to be persuaded to come to the aid of Greece and Turkey, President Truman prepared a speech

---

[1] McCullough, *Truman*, 539-541

to outline the importance of aiding nations who struggled against communism.[2] Adding an element of difficulty to Truman's sales pitch to Congress was the downsizing of the United States military which had shrunk form 12 million men in 1945 to 1.6 million in 1947.[3] Time was running out for action, however, according to the president's advisors. A serious blow to the policy of containment was possibly only a short time away with Greece teetering on the brink of being overwhelmed by communist guerillas.[4] After consideration, President Truman decided it was in the nation's best interest to assist Greece and Turkey. The next step was convincing Congress of the necessity of actions and the implications of failing to curb the extension of the Soviet sphere.

President Truman delivered a speech to Congress on March 12, 1947 in which he not only laid out the importance of American assistance to Greece and Turkey, but also verbally outlined what would become known as the Truman Doctrine.[5] One section of the speech outlined Truman's vision for American intervention to successfully contain communism. Starting with Greece and Turkey, the president said, "I believe that it must be the policy of the United States to support free peoples who are resisting attempted

---

[2] Ibid., 542-547.
[3] John Lewis Gaddis, *Strategies of Containment: A Critical Appraisal of American National Security Policy during the Cold War* (Oxford: Oxford University Press, 2005), 23.
[4] Ibid., 539-547.
[5] Ibid., 547.

subjugation by armed minorities or by outside pressures. I believe that we must assist free peoples to work out their own destinies in their own way. I believe that our help should be primarily through economic and financial aid which is essential to economic stability and orderly political processes."[6] The United States would commit itself to containment by coming to aid of any nation struggling against the desired increase in the communist domain.

With specific reference to ongoing situation in Greece, the president told Congress, "The very existence of the Greek state is today threatened by the terrorist activities of several thousand armed men, led by Communists, who defy the government's authority at a number of points, particularly along the northern boundaries…Greece must have assistance if it is to become a self-supporting and self-respecting democracy. The United States must supply this assistance."[7]

As the president's speech reached its climax, he brought the realities of what it would mean to the United States and the Free World if America failed at that moment. Truman drove home his message speaking, "Should we fail to aid Greece and Turkey in this fateful hour, the effect will be far reaching to the West as well as to the East. We must take immediate and resolute action…The

---

[6] "Public Papers of the Presidents: Harry S. Truman 1945-1953. 56. Special Message to the Congress on Greece and Turkey: The Truman Doctrine." Harry S. Truman Library and Museum. Accessed February 3, 2017.

[7] Ibid.

free peoples of the world look to us for support in maintaining their freedoms. If we falter in our leadership, we may endanger the peace of the world—and we shall surely endanger the welfare of this Nation."[8]

The price tag for action in Greece and Turkey would cost more than what the American taxpayer had been asked to pay to defeat the Axis Powers in World War II. The recently ended war had cost the United States roughly $341 billion while the estimated aid to Greece and Turkey hovered around the $400 billion mark.[9] The president was determined in his conviction that failing to act at that moment would cost America vastly more in American blood and dollars later than he was asking in aid.[10]

---

8   Ibid.
9   McCullough, *Truman*, 548.
10 Ibid.

V

The Iron Curtain Descends

A year before the announcement of the Truman Doctrine, and only two weeks following the Long Telegram[1], the emerging Cold War was put into words that were easily understandable to people of all walks of life. Former British Prime Minister Winston Churchill defined the growing Cold War during a speech to an American audience in March of 1946.[2] Churchill was on vacation in the United States when word reached him that a college in Fulton Missouri wanted to give him an honorary degree. President Harry S. Truman told Churchill that he would join him for the journey to Missouri and sponsor the speech. Having the president of the United States sponsor a private citizen like Churchill was at the time following his removal from the post he held in the British

---

1   Ben Steil, *The Marshall Plan: Dawn of the Cold War* (New York: Simon and Schuster, 2018), 10.
2   Robert H. Ferrell, *Harry S. Truman: A Life* (Columbia: University of Missouri Press, 1994.), 234-235.

government during World War II, was not only an honor, but also slightly out of character for Harry Truman.[3]

Churchill left his vacation in Florida and made the journey to Missouri with the president.[4] Since Missouri was the home state of Harry Truman, the speech carried a certain level of significance appearing to have the president's blessing. Arriving at Westminster College, Churchill had a goal in mind with his speech and that was to make the average American citizen aware of the growing threat of the Soviet Union in Europe.[5] Churchill addressed the assembled crowd with ominous warning and dramatic flair driving home the suffering taking place throughout post-war Europe speaking, "The awful ruin of Europe, with all its vanished glories, and of large parts of Asia glares us in the eyes. When the designs of wicked men or the aggressive urge of mighty States dissolve over large areas the frame of civilised society, humble folk are confronted with difficulties with which they cannot cope. For them all is distorted, all is broken, even ground to pulp…When I stand here this quiet afternoon I shudder to visualise what is actually happening to millions now and what is going to happen in this period when famine stalks the earth. None can compute what has been called "the unestimated sum of human pain." Our supreme task and duty is to guard the homes of the common

---

3   Ibid.
4   Ibid.
5   Ibid.

people from the horrors and miseries of another war. We are all agreed on that."[6]

Winston Churchill then took direct aim at the Soviet Union. He called the communists out by name and addressed them as the creators of potential chaos inside a war-torn Europe saying, "A shadow has fallen upon the scenes so lately lighted by the Allied victory. Nobody knows what Soviet Russia and its Communist international organisation intends to do in the immediate future, or what are the limits, if any, to their expansive and proselytising tendencies."[7]

In the most famous passage of the speech which was officially titled "The Sinews of Peace," Churchill uttered a phrase that gave the speech its more common name. Referred to throughout the years as "The Iron Curtain Speech," the former prime minister painted a picture of a Europe separated by an iron curtain. On one side of the division was the parcel of the continent dedicated to freedom and self-government after the defeat of Hitler. To the east, Europe was under the clutches of a new form of totalitarianism dedicated to a selfish land grab in the aftermath of the Second World War. Making this point, Churchill informed the Missouri

---

[6] "The Sinews of Peace ('Iron Curtain Speech')." The International Churchill Society. April 13, 2017. Accessed March 23, 2018. https://www.winstonchurchill.org/resources/speeches/1946-1963-elder-statesman/the-sinews-of-peace/

[7] Ibid.

audience, "From Stettin in the Baltic to Trieste in the Adriatic, an iron curtain has descended across the Continent. Behind that line lie all the capitals of the ancient states of Central and Eastern Europe. Warsaw, Berlin, Prague, Vienna, Budapest, Belgrade, Bucharest and Sofia, all these famous cities and the populations around them lie in what I must call the Soviet sphere, and all are subject in one form or another, not only to Soviet influence but to a very high and, in many cases, increasing measure of control from Moscow. Athens alone-Greece with its immortal glories-is free to decide its future at an election under British, American and French observation. The Russian-dominated Polish Government has been encouraged to make enormous and wrongful inroads upon Germany, and mass expulsions of millions of Germans on a scale grievous and undreamed-of are now taking place. The Communist parties, which were very small in all these Eastern States of Europe, have been raised to pre-eminence and power far beyond their numbers and are seeking everywhere to obtain totalitarian control. Police governments are prevailing in nearly every case, and so far, except in Czechoslovakia, there is no true democracy." [8]

In some regards, the speech echoed the words of George F. Kennan's telegram from the previous month. On the other hand, Churchill's words made a relation with wartime ally Joseph

---

8   Ibid.

Stalin more difficult. Even President Truman claimed not to have seen the speech previous to the day Churchill delivered the words at Westminster College and even went as far as to offer Stalin the opportunity to make his own speech in America.[9] Either way, the words spoken by Churchill only further defined the dire circumstances ongoing in Europe. The Soviet Union was not interested in allowing the nations freed by its army to follow the path of self-government and was still dedicated to the march of communism around the globe. Future cooperation between the United States and the Soviet Union was starting to be acknowledged as impractical and impossible.

---

9   Ferrell, *Harry S. Truman*, 235.

VI

The Marshall Plan and National Security

The turnaround from one Cold War crisis to another would prove swift for President Truman in the early years of a post–World War II world. Now that the administration had a solid policy foundation on which to rely, international events seemed to have a desire to test the Truman administration and the policy of containment. History would go on to record the Truman years as an era of action that required extraordinary creativity, ingenuity, and determination from American leaders saddled with the responsibility of defending free peoples from the global plans of the Soviet Union and communism.

Truman's Secretary of State, George Marshall, introduced what would become the European Recovery Act during a commencement address at Harvard University in 1947. Adding a humanitarian arm to the policy of containment, Truman adopted Marshall's call for the United States to aid the worn-torn countries of Europe. Truman and Marshall hoped that if the United States sent economic aid to the decimated nations of Europe, then democracy could be saved on the continent.[1] World history has been littered with stories of dire economic conditions leading people to accept extreme governments in exchange for daily sustenance. The United States earnestly wanted to keep such events from happening again.

The terrible conditions throughout Europe following World War II were almost beyond comprehension. As the Allies celebrated the surrender of Nazi Germany on May 8, 1945, Germany itself and much of Europe was unrecognizable to anyone who had seen the continent's beauty before the war. There had never been a war as destructive as the Second World War. In its wake, the continent of Europe was consumed with death, starvation, turmoil and ruin. Complicating matters even further was the Soviet Union's readiness to pounce on the unstable situation and expand its own borders and influence farther than the previously agreed on boundaries.[2]

Following World War II, 27 million Soviets had disappeared as casualties of the conflict. In Germany, over 5 million soldiers had been killed in the fighting with an additional million-plus civilians killed

---

[1] William J. Bennett, America: The Last Best Hope: Volume II: From a World at War to the Triumph of Freedom (Nashville: Thomas Nelson, 2007), 277.

[2] *After Hitler*, Directed by David Korn-Brzoza. Produced by Fabienne Servan Schreiber and Luci pastor. France Television, 2016.

from Allied bombing raids and other war-related tragedies. France had seen the destruction of thousands of buildings, large portions of Holland was under water due to dams being destroyed, and the over 6 million Jewish corpses of Hitler's genocide were constantly being found. In all, over 40 million Europeans died in World War II leaving the continent in almost utter ruin. Adding to the severity of the situation was the millions of refugees searching for suitable living conditions and the millions of Axis POWs still being held by the Allies.[3]

Europe was definitely being overwhelmed by the post war problems it faced when Secretary Marshall announced the plan to rebuild Europe. The European Recovery Act would become more commonly referred to as the Marshall Plan due to George Marshall being the mastermind behind the plan. On the day he outlined the basis of what would become the European Recovery Act, Marshall spoke to the Harvard crowd, "Our policy is…against hunger, poverty, desperation and chaos. Its purpose should be the revival of a working economy in the world so as to permit the emergence of political and social conditions in which free institutions can exist."[4] The Truman administration was committed to helping Europeans emerge from the rubble of a world war, and set the continent on a path toward being a peaceful coexistence of democratic neighbors.

---

3   Ibid.
4   McCullough, *Truman*, 563.

The United States of America was venturing into new and uncharted territory for the nation by announcing the Marshall Plan. The U.S. had a history of being cautious when entering into anything that could be viewed as a foreign entanglement. Dating as far back a George Washington's farewell address warning against getting too involved in foreign affairs, the U.S. had tried to maintain a separation from the rest of the world as best as it could. Now, Americans were coming to the realization that their country was a nation deeply involved in the affairs of other nations. The success of the United States depended on the success of Europe and Asia which meant economic investments around the world to stabilize the post-war economy, as well an almost constant military presence, were needed to stop the spread of communism.[5]

A few months after Marshall's address at Harvard, the United States government decided a restructuring of departments was necessary to strengthen national security. The National Security Act of 1947 went into effect on July 26, 1947. In the act, new government agencies were created such as the Central Intelligence Agency and Department of Defense, as well as a new military structure that streamlined the armed forces into one command structure. The opening of the newly written National Security Act stated it was: "An Act To promote the national security by providing for a Secretary of Defense; for a National Military

---

5   Steil, *The Marshall Plan*, 1-13.

Establishment; for a Department of the Army, a Department of the Navy, and a Department of the Air Force; and for the coordination of the activities of the National Military Establishment with other departments and agencies of the Government concerned with the national security."[6] National security was now of the utmost importance in the face of the growing communist enemy; even during a time of peace.

---

6 "National Security Act of 1947." Office of the Director of National Intelligence. Accessed February 10, 2017. www.dni.gov

VII

Standing Firm in Berlin

A year following the unveiling of the Marshall Plan and the National Security Act, President Harry S. Truman faced reelection by the American people. As the campaign season approached, he led the nation through one of the first major direct face-offs with the Soviet Union of the Cold War. The Soviet Union cut off all rail and road access to Berlin, Germany on June 24, 1948.[1] Stalin had basically isolated West Berlin. The free sector of the German capital was now completely encircled by communist-controlled territory cutting off all major ground access to the city. Defying the advice of some of his advisors, President Truman decided to make a stand in Berlin.[2] The United States would not abandon its allies.

---

1   Margaret Truman, *Harry S. Truman* (New York: William Morrow & Company, Inc., 1973), 12.
2   Ibid.

It appeared to President Truman that war might be becoming more likely as the Berlin Blockade began.³ Searching for ways to keep the city supplied with essential materials during the blockade, the entry of supplies through the air became the most likely means of success.⁴ If the United States did not act, over 2,000,000 Germans living in Berlin could face death by starvation.⁵ Early on the United States used any airplane they could find to supply the stranded Berliners,⁶ making it clear the United States was up to the challenge brought to them by apparent Soviet aggression.

Many in the press had voiced their displeasure in the past about the United States and the western allies not driving into Berlin during the last days of Hitler's Germany in 1945. Critics claimed the United States could have rescued more of Germany, including its capital city, from the Red Army. Some of this criticism was directed toward the Yalta agreements but General Dwight Eisenhower received his fair share of disparagement about the U.S. not taking Berlin.⁷ Occasionally, Eisenhower would later have to defend his Berlin decision as president or during his campaigns. Those who were angered over the United States allowing the Soviets to drive that deep into Germany now had the

---

3   Ibid.
4   Andrei Cherny, *The Candy Bombers: The Untold Story of the Berlin Airlift and America's Finest Hour* (New York: The Berkley Publishing Group, 2008), 251.
5   Ibid., 250-251.
6   Ibid., 253
7   Paul Johnson, *Eisenhower: A Life* (New York: Penguin Books, 2014), 52-57.

opportunity to feel vindicated as news of Stalin's blockade rang out through the world.

Faced with what could be the start of a war with the Soviet Union or the destruction of the prestige of the United States throughout the world, President Truman decided a calculated, firm response was the best approach. Stalin clearly played the role of the villain in the eyes of the free world by using human lives and a city in his game of chess against the west. The Truman Administration built the perfect response to the crisis that would keep the city alive while standing up to communist aggression.

Throughout the blockade, American bombers kept the city alive with vital supplies that the people of Berlin were incapable of attaining in any other way. Often, the same planes that had been used to bomb Berlin during World War II were now used to sustain the city as the Stalin tried to strangle it away from the western powers. With unprecedented logistics and fierce determination, President Truman, the United States, and its allies shocked Stalin with their ability to keep the city stocked with supplies during the Blockade.[8] Truman's decision to match the communist challenge in Berlin proved successful in stopping that particular avenue of Soviet aggression and avoiding a full-scale war with the Soviet Union. Stalin had no choice but to revoke the blockade in

---

8   John Lewis Gaddis, *We Now Know: Rethinking Cold War History* (Oxford: Oxford University Press, 1997), 48.

May of 1949.⁹ The United States of America had successfully emerged from this first part of a dangerous international game that unfortunately had many more innings left to play.

The reasons why Stalin attempted the blockade of Berlin are not entirely clear but his actions do seem to have some connection to the unveiling of the Marshall Plan. It is likely he was trying to hinder consolidation efforts of the American, French, and British sectors into one West German nation. Stalin may have also believed he could force those three nations completely out of Germany. Whatever his motives were, Harry Truman's strong insistence on helping the people of West Berlin resulted in a boost in positive perception of the United States among the German people, as well as a loss of prestige in the region for Stalin.¹⁰ The limited approach of containment for dealing with the communist threat avoided World War III, proving containment to be a sound tactic as long as the United States could possess the persistence necessary to make it work. The result of the Berlin Airlift was that the United States had successfully contained communism.

---

9   Ibid.
10 Gaddis, *The Cold War*, 33-34.

VIII

Losing the Atomic Monopoly

The biggest advantage the United States possessed in the attempt to stop the spread of communism was its monopoly on atomic weaponry. The U.S. was the only nation on earth to have nuclear capabilities in its arsenal, and the country was led by the only person in history who had ordered the use of the bomb in world history. This greatly tilted the balance of military power in favor of the United States. The Soviet Union did not possess any weapon capable of matching the effectiveness of the atomic bomb in the early days of the Cold War putting the communist world at an extreme disadvantage.[1] Losing the full competitive edge on atomic weapons was unthinkable to some Americans. But if it ever occurred, it would send panicked shockwaves throughout the western world.

The atomic monopoly, and thereby all potential future success of containment, was delivered a serious setback in 1949. Intelligence

---

1   Gaddis, *Strategies of Containment*, 60-61.

gathering agencies believed the United States had sizable cushion of time remaining as the world's sole possessor of nuclear arms when news broke of the Soviet Union's first successful testing of the bomb. By the Soviet Union added this mega weapon to its military, the Truman administration had to come to terms with the leveling of the Cold War playing field. President Truman had to wonder whether containment was now the best option in dealing with the growing communist threat since the U.S.S.R. had developed the basis of first-strike capabilities.

The detonation of an atomic bomb by the Soviet Union unleashed a wave of Cold War mania throughout the United States. Americans had long held to a deep-rooted fear of communist subterfuge as a nation, but Soviet ownership of a nuclear weapon heightened those fears to a new level. The Cold War would forever be altered into a nervous time of bomb shelters and air-raid preparations.

Part II

1950–1956

"There is no substitute for victory."
–General Douglas MacArthur

I

Spies and McCarthy

Adding to the anxiety gripping the United States was the revelation that the Soviets may have been aided from American citizens in their successful quest to pursue the bomb. As the 1940s came to a close, scientist Klaus Fuchs admitted he had been spying for the Soviet Union while working on the American Manhattan Project to build the atomic bomb.[1] His confession coincided with the perjury conviction of Alger Hiss. While under oath, former U.S. State Department employee Hiss claimed he was not guilty of being a Soviet spy.[2] Testimonies against Hiss led the U.S. government to come to the opinion that he had lied under oath and was guilty of espionage. Combined with the convictions of Julius and Ethel Rosenberg for giving highly classified atomic

---

1   Gaddis, *The Cold War: A New History* (New York: Penguin Group, 2005), 39.
2   Ibid.

secrets to the Soviets,³ a very tense and real panic was gripping the United States.

In addition to the shocking news of potential spies living amongst them, the speed at which communism was racking up victories around the globe became a growing reason of concern for Americans. Questions about how the Soviets gathered the necessary information to build an atomic bomb, combined with similar inquiries about the speedy rise of communism in China, caused many citizens to wonder if the United States was on the right path. Increasing numbers of Americans began to wonder if the possibility of leaks inside the government existed. One person who believed communists were not only obtaining information from, but infiltrating the highest levels of the U.S. government was Wisconsin Senator Joseph McCarthy.[4]

In early 1950, Joseph McCarthy addressed a group of Republican voters in Wheeling, West Virginia. His speech that February day to the Women's Republican Club of Wheeling, West Virginia would move the Senator out of obscurity and into the forefront of the increasing suspicion movement growing inside Cold War America.[5] During the speech, McCarthy made allegations before the crowd that transfixed his audience, as well as the nation, with the persuasive power of paranoia. He claimed to have the names of "card carrying

---

3   Walter Isaacson, *Einstein: His Life and Universe* (New York: Simon and Schuster Paperbacks, 2007), 525.
4   Ibid., 40.
5   Ibid.

members… of the communist party" in his hand of people who had infiltrated the highest levels of the U.S. government.[6]

The Truman administration spent considerable time and effort trying to debunk the claims of Senator McCarthy in early 1950.[7] McCarthy had claimed there were 57 communist party members working inside the United States State Department. The accusation was earnestly denied by the State Department. President Truman supported the State Department's claim of innocence while appearing dismissive of Senator McCarthy's claims during his February 16, 1950 press conference. When asked about the Senator's charges, the president answered, "I think the State Department answered that by saying there was not a work of truth in the Senator said."[8] Even though Truman had access to the presidential bully pulpit, it would take more than presidential support of accused government officials with pleas of innocence to rid America of the hysteria brought on by Senator Joseph McCarthy. McCarthy's reign of terror had just begun and the senator would not easily surrender his new found fame.

---

6   Bennett, *America: The Last Best Hope: Volume II: From a World at War to the Triumph of Freedom* (Nashville: Thomas Nelson), 303
7   Gaddis, *The Cold War*, 40.
8   "Public Papers of the Presidents: Harry S. Truman 1945-1953. 38. President's News Conference." Harry S. Truman Library and Museum. Accessed January 24, 2017.

II

Trouble in Korea

In the midst of the McCarthy hysteria, the Cold War showed no signs of slowing down. Arguably, the biggest test for President Truman and the policy of containment came in the form of communist aggression in an unlikely part of the world. The Korean peninsula was not considered high on the priority list for the Truman administration as a place where a Cold War conflict could arise. When North Korean communists attacked South Korean forces on June 25, 1950, the United States now had to decide how much it was willing to risk to stop communism in Asia. Did the United States have the resources, the manpower, and the resolve to fight a war against communism to save South Korea in 1950? The answer from President Truman would be a firm "yes."

Communist forces had fought their way to power in China a year before the trouble in Korea. News of Mao Zedong, who had risen to power among Chinese communists in the 1930s,[1] claiming power over the Chinese Nationalist forces added to the bad press hitting the Truman administration. Add the China situation to the Soviet development of an atomic bomb, and President Truman was facing a political firestorm that would force his hand into dealing with communism in Korea. Mao's forces achieved victory in China only a week after the Soviet Union detonated its first atomic bomb.[2] With the strengthening of Soviet military capabilities and appearances of losing Asia to communism becoming a startling reality, Truman couldn't afford to allow the whole Korean peninsula to fall under the control of the communist aggressors. If for nothing other than political purposes, he had to act decisively. The president realized communism was on the march, and the unfamiliar Korean peninsula was another location where the policy of containment had to be applied.

The Japanese army had occupied the Korean peninsula until the end of World War II. As with the division of Germany after the defeat of Hitler's forces, the Korean peninsula was divided between the United States and the Soviet Union. The location chosen for the dividing line was the 38th parallel, which contained no real significance other than the fact it was a convenient line

---

1   Archie Brown, *The Rise and Fall of Communism*, (New York: HarperCollins Publishers, 2009), 100.
2   Gibbs and Duffy, *The President's Club: Inside the World's Most Exclusive Fraternity* (New York: Simon and Schuster paperbacks, 2012), 66

upon the map. Future Secretary of State under President Kennedy, and Assistant Secretary of State for Far Eastern Affairs for Harry S. Truman, Dean Rusk handled the U.S. negotiations in the division of the peninsula after World War II.[3]

Considerable attention had not been paid to Korea after World War II. With this in mind, the movement of North Korean combat forces over the 38th parallel appeared to take the United States government completely by surprise.[4] Even President Harry Truman was enjoying a vacation at his home in Missouri when he received word of the beginning of hostilities. Secretary of State Dean Acheson called the president with the pressing news of the situation in Korea saying, "Mr. President, I have very serious news. The North Koreans have invaded South Korea."[5] Secretary Acheson also informed the president that he called an emergency meeting of the United Nations Security Council to discuss the issue.[6]

At the time of the North Korean invasion, the highest-ranking American officer in the Pacific was General Douglas MacArthur. He was stationed in Tokyo at the time as the leader of the American

---

[3] Arthur Herman, Douglas *MacArthur: American Warrior* (New York: Random House, 2016), 636-637.
[4] McCullough, *Truman* (New York: Simon and Schuster Paperbacks, 1992), 777.
[5] Ibid., 774-775.
[6] Ibid., 775.

occupation of Japan after World War II.[7] The news of the Korean conflict even appeared to take MacArthur by surprise. He was awaken in the early morning hours of June 25th and informed of the situation. President Truman would soon be looking to General MacArthur to lead American soldiers, and the forces of the United Nations, to repel the North Korean communist invasion.

President Truman was beginning to see North Korea as another totalitarian state like the ones that caused the outbreak of World War II, and he wanted to stop them before they reached the levels of a Hitler or a Mussolini.[8] The United Nations appeared to agree with Truman's assessment of the situation. The U.N. Security Council passed an American resolution calling for an end to hostilities and for North Korean forces to return north of the 38th parallel before Truman arrived back in Washington, D.C.[9] The Soviet Union had refused to attend the U.N. meeting as a protest over the United States position on China and Formosa. Upon arriving back in the nation's capital, the president gave General MacArthur his official permission to send military support to South Korea.[10] At the same time, Truman ordered the United

---

7   John Lewis Gaddis, *The Cold War*, 41.
8   Arthur Herman, *Douglas MacArthur*, 713.
9   McCullough, *Truman*, 777.
10 Herman, *Douglas MacArthur*, 713.

States navy to Formosa to protect against any further possible communist action in the area.[11]

President Truman believed that the events in Korea provided a perfect opportunity for the United States to stand against Soviet aggression. It became the firm position of his administration that the North Koreans must be stopped. Truman realized he had to take a tough stand against North Korea. He couldn't afford to be the president who "lost" China to communism, was at the wheel when the Soviets developed the bomb, and stood by as communism overtook the entire Korean peninsula. Now, the only real questions left was how far the United States would go in defense of South Korea and how could the U.S. protect its ally without provoking a response from the Soviet Union. An entry of Soviet troops into Korea would increase the likelihood of an outbreak of World War III and the spreading of war around the globe.[12]

With tensions in Asia adding to increased fears of the Cold War standoff going nuclear, Truman called upon an American hero to bring stability to the new North Atlantic Treaty Organization (NATO). The organization had been created as a mutual defense among anti-communist countries to protect against communist hostility. NATO was only a year old when fighting broke out in Korea. General Dwight D. Eisenhower was called upon to lead the

---

11 Ibid.
12 McCullough, *Truman*, 777-780

armed branch of NATO partly due to his status as champion of the European theater of World War II. The communist were going on the offensive and every roadblock to their expansion was now necessary.[13] At the time, no one could accurately predict if Korea was an isolated pocket of communist aggression or a smaller piece to a larger puzzle. NATO had been formed with the intentions of keeping Western Europe collectively safe from communism.[14] Now with the communist on the move around the world, having General Eisenhower at the helm helped ease the fears of Europeans who sensed a war may soon be coming to their continent.

Initially, American military operations in Korea were not successful. The South Koreans proved to be an unreliable ally who often scattered at the sounds of approaching enemy tanks. The United States had to deal with fielding an army after the post-World War II downsizing that had drastically reduced the number of available men and machinery.[15] The North Koreans had essentially taken control of most of the Korean peninsula[16] and appeared to be an almost unstoppable force in the early days of the conflict.

The U.S./U.N. forces would eventually gain the upper hand after General Douglas MacArthur convinced his superiors to

---

13 Gibbs and Duffy. *The President's Club*, 68.
14 Bennett, *America: The Last Best Hope*, 295.
15 Herman, *MacArthur*, 713.
16 Gaddis, *The Cold War*, 43.

allow him to proceed with a daring amphibious invasion of the Korean peninsula. MacArthur's plan was to land behind the main communist forces and cut their lines of communication and supply. With an invasion fleet of over 200 vessels, MacArthur's forces landed at Inchon behind enemy lines on September 15, 1950.[17] Preceded by a bombardment of North Korean defenses, the invasion was an overwhelming success for the United States and the United Nations. [18]

General Douglas MacArthur had turned the tide of the war in favor of the anti-communist alliance. The communist forces were quickly driven mile after mile closer to the 38th parallel. The American-led victories were so crushing to the enemy that MacArthur convinced the Truman administration American soldiers would be home by Christmas.[19] The United States of America appeared to have successfully stood up to communism in its first armed conflict with the aggressors.

MacArthur's forces picked up one victory after another over the North Koreans and began pushing the communists back over the 38th parallel. Everything was going according to U.S. plans after the landing at Inchon. The feelings of a quick ending to the conflict in Korea however, came to an abrupt end when U.S. and

---

[17] H.W. Brands, *The General and the President: MacArthur and Truman at the Brink of Nuclear War* (New York: Doubleday, 2016), 159-160.

[18] Ibid.

[19] Herman, *MacArthur*, 751-754.

U.N. soldiers encountered an enemy battalion in an unfamiliar uniform. Not only was the structure of the conflict on the Korean peninsula about to change, but the face of warfare in the 20th Century would be forever altered.

The leader of Communist China, Mao Zedong, prepared his military for action against MacArthur's forces if the United Nations military units crossed the 38th parallel.[20] In October of 1950, the Chinese army struck American, South Korean, and British military units as they were closing in on ridding the peninsula of all communist combat units. The anti-communist forces were quickly beaten by this new foe who came at them with a completely new style of fighting. They slowed the U.N. advance with a series of roadblocks and ambushes. Bloodied, tired, confused, and freezing in the harsh Korean winter climate, U.N. soldiers fell back decisively beaten. China had entered the war.

No one in the Truman administration wanted the conflict in Korea to spread. Ever present was the fear of Soviet intervention, or the possibility of a widespread communist offensive blossoming into World War III. With Chinese troops now joining the battle in Korea, the war had grown from a Korean conflict to a regional struggle with communism. President Truman wanted to proceed

---

20 Bevin Alexander, *MacArthur's War: The Flawed Genius who Challenged the American Political System* (New York: Berkeley Publishing Group, 2013), 121.

with caution as every action could now be the move that unleashed a third global war in less than 40 years.

President Truman explained the American position in Korea on April 11, 1951. In the Report to the American People on Korea, the president reiterated the point about trying to keep the conflict from spreading and creating a third world war. Truman told the American people, "I want to talk to you plainly tonight about what we are doing in Korea and about our policy in the Far East. In the simplest terms, what we are doing in Korea is this: We are trying to prevent a third world war."[21] The president framed the issue of Korea in clear cold war terminology telling the American public, "The Communist in the Kremlin are engaged in a monstrous conspiracy to stamp out freedom all over the world. If they were to succeed, the United States would be numbered among their principle victims. It must be clear to everyone that the United States cannot – and will not-sit idly by and await foreign conquest. The only question is: What is the best time to meet the threat and how is the best way to meet it? The best time to meet the threat is in the beginning."[22]

The objective for President Truman was now finding a way to get American troops out of Korea without completely abandoning South Korea. In addition, he needed to put a lid on this war

---

[21] David Krugler, ed., *The Cold War: Core Documents* (Ashland: Ashbrook Center, 2018) 38.

[22] Ibid.

before it grew out of control while still containing communism. The Truman administration was not in a position to eradicate communism due to adopting containment as its preferred method of dealing with the communist threat.[23]

Then, a constitutional problem arose over General Douglas MacArthur's belief in winning any conflict the United States was engaged in by complete destruction of the enemy. MacArthur's view of how things should be handled in Korea placed him in direct conflict with the constitutionally sanctioned chain of command inside the U.S. government. MacArthur believed U.S. military operations in Korea were left shackled by containment's philosophy of avoiding conflict and the limiting of the scope of conflict when it did arise.[24] Often, the general would publicly share his criticisms of President Truman in a manner that threatened the precedent of civilian control of the military.

President Truman finally made the decision to remove General MacArthur from his position in the Army's Far East Theater. The president and his administration came to the conclusion that MacArthur's approach to handling the increasingly complex situation in Asia was no longer the proper path to pursue. More importantly, President Truman finally agreed with his Washington colleagues' assessment that MacArthur was a dangerous man and

---

23 Alexander, *MacArthur's War*, 4.
24 Ibid., 5.

his preferred approach to the conflict would end in devastation for the United States. It became ever more apparent that if MacArthur would have his way in Korea, the conflict would escalate into World War III. MacArthur's path might even lead to the introduction of atomic weapons in Asia. Therefore, he had to go.

In the congressional hearing that followed the firing of MacArthur, the Truman policy of restrained containment was put on trial against MacArthur's strategy of broader warfare that would have utilized the full capabilities of the U.S. army against the communist enemy. It became clear in the hearings that MacArthur's plans of using troops from Formosa in Korea, and bombing Chinese supply lines in Korea and China would have led to a wider war with Red China. This would have possibly even led the Soviet Union to join the fighting. Truman's Secretary of Defense explained the administration's fear of escalation at the hearings when he stated, "General MacArthur, on the other hand, would have us, on our own initiative, carry the conflict beyond Korea against the mainland of Communist China… He would've accepted this risk of involvement not only in an extension of war with Red China but in an all-out war with the Soviet Union. He would have done this even at the expense of losing our allies and wrecking the coalition of free peoples throughout the world. He would have us do this even though the effect of such action might expose Western Europe to attack by the millions of Soviet troops poised in Middle and Eastern Europe."[25] Chairman of the Joint Chiefs of Staff, Omar Bradley, also added similar sentiments in favor of the administration's limited war goals of containment and against MacArthur's expansion of conflict.[26]

It was not an ideal time to dismiss the top commander at the height of the first armed conflict with communism of the Cold War. Also, MacArthur remained extremely popular at home. His dismissal erased any glimmer of a chance of Truman staying on for a third term,[27] especially when it was revealed how MacArthur, the national war hero had unceremoniously learned of his dismissal.[28] The historical importance of the dismissal of MacArthur is found in the fact that Truman was not going to allow the U.S. Constitution to become a casualty of the Cold War. Acting as the elected commander-in-chief of the republic, Truman did not let the desire to contain communism undermine the properly defined roles of the constitution. Even though the United States found itself in a new position of global importance after World War II, the constitutional idea of civilian leadership of the military would remain intact.

---

25 Brands, *The General vs. the President*, 355.
26 Ibid. 359-362.
27 Ibid., 311-313.
28 Ibid., 305-308.

III

Duck and Cover

The Korean War proved to many that the fears of communism as a threat to the security of the world were not just unfounded paranoia. Communism was indeed on the move. In just the short span of a year, China had fallen to communism, South Korea had been attacked by communists, and the Soviet Union had successfully detonated an atomic bomb. The threat was real and no one could accurately predict when and if the threat would end. A direct conflict with the Soviet Union was growing likely in the minds of many Americans. With this growing threat, Americans began to prepare themselves for the potential of a Soviet strike on the homeland that may include atomic bombs. As it would remain throughout the duration of the Cold War, the fear of atomic weapons falling from the sky onto American cities and citizens proved to be an ever-present concern.

The United States government had been investigating the potential terror of an atomic bomb landing inside the United States as far back as 1946. Three years before the Soviet Union would catch up with the U.S. and remove its atomic monopoly, an American bombing survey looked into what citizens of the U.S. could expect if America ever faced the type of destruction dropped on Nagasaki and Hiroshima at the conclusion of World War II.[1] It was no secret to the world that the atomic weapon had transformed warfare and brought dangerous new machines of war into existence that now lived in the daily lives of Americans thanks to the Cold War.

The report began by stating a serious and somber question, "What if the target for the bomb had been an American city?"[2] Answering this question, the report looked into what had actually increased the odds of survival during the atomic blasts and what structures received the least amount of damage from the bomb. The first finding of the report was that shelters were essential to surviving a nuclear attack stating, "the most instructive fact at Nagasaki was the survival, even when near ground zero, of the few hundred people who were properly placed in the tunnel shelters. Carefully built shelters, though unoccupied, stood up well in both cities. Without question, shelters can protect those who get to them against anything but a direct hit. Adequate warning will assure that a maximum number get to shelters." [3]

Along with shelters, the report stated that the United States would need to create a civilian defense system to protect from a

---

1   Keane, ed., *World War II Documents* (Ashland: Ashbrook Center, 2018), 157.
2   Ibid.
3   Ibid.

nuclear strike. Spelling out the need for a civil defense apparatus, the report stated, "Because the scale of disaster would be certain to overwhelm the locality in which it occurs, mutual assistance organized on a national level is essential…highly trained mobile units skilled in and equipped for fire-fighting, rescue work, and clearance and repair should be trained for an emergency which disrupts local organization and exceeds its capability for control."[4] In this survey of World War II bombing report, the origins of the Cold War civil defense programs were born.[5]

To address the threat of atomic weapons potentially being used on the U.S. population, a civil defense film was created to acquaint Americans with skills necessary to potentially surviving a nuclear attack was produced. In the short film called "Duck and Cover," school children are taught what to do if they see a bright flash or hear the air raid sirens sounding the alarm to alert the dangers of an incoming atomic bomb. With the help of "Bert the Turtle," a cartoon character who stars in the short film, American children were given a lesson on surviving an attack.[6]

Throughout the film, children face various scenarios in which their town or school is attacked. They always follow the advice of the cartoon turtle and "duck and cover." Whether they are in

---

4   Ibid., 159.
5   Ibid., 157.
6   Duck and Cover (1951) Bert the Turtle. YouTube. Accessed March 13, 2018. https://www.youtube.com/watch?v=IKqXu-5jw60

class, at home, in the hallway, the cafeteria, or playing outside, the children are taught to get into a building if possible. If a building is not available, they are to "duck and cover" away from the blast for protection.[7] Millions of Americans watched this film and the others produced during the Cold War dealing with a potential atomic bomb attack. Films like "Duck and Cover" illustrated how the threat of the bomb was ever-present and Americans now had to stay vigilant at all times to survive the potential war with communist forces.

Even with education about how to survive a potential attack, the likelihood of surviving such an event was still low as pointed out to the readers of a 1950 Civil Defense booklet. The booklet asked its readers the question: What are you chances?[8] Answering that deadly serious question was the response, "If a modern A-bomb exploded without warning in the air over your home town tonight, your calculated chances of living through the raid would run something like this: Should you happen to be one of the unlucky people right under the bomb, there is practically no hope of living through it. In fact, anywhere within one-half mile of the center of the explosion, your chances of escaping are about 1 out of 10."[9] Even with these sobering facts, the booklet did paint an optimistic picture of the

---

7   Ibid.
8   U.S. Department of Defense, *Civil Defense Booklets: Volume 2, The Red dog Nuclear Survival Series* (Red Dog Press, Inc.: 2010), 2.
9   Ibid.

potential for surviving an A-bomb if you were more than 2 miles away from the blast.[10]

Americans had to live with these fears during the first fifteen years of the Cold War and beyond. As bombs became more powerful and the means to deliver them became more efficient, increased measures were needed to protect Americans from the war that seemed inevitable. Even the New Yorker painted a scary picture in 1955 in article titled *Fallout* that explained the long lasting dangers of atomic weaponry claiming that fallout from the first testing blast in New Mexico caused radiation to show up in corn as far away as Indiana.[11] With spies potentially lurking throughout the American homeland and the Soviet Union successful completion of an A-bomb, fear grew as communism expanded around the globe. Death could fall from the sky at any moment.

---

10 Ibid., 3.
11 Henry Finder, ed., *The 50s: The Story of a Decade* (New York: random House, 2015), 11

IV

The End of the Truman Years

As the Truman presidency came to a close, the popularity of the president had been damaged by the stalemate in Korea, the expansion of communism in China, the Soviet development of the atomic bomb, and the firing of America's beloved general, Douglas MacArthur. It would take several years for history to save the legacy of Harry S. Truman as one of the main architects in the successful American struggle against communism. The American public in 1952-53 failed to see greatness in Harry Truman. All that the public saw then was a man who had failed to beat the communists. It was time for a new president to live in the White House with experience in war, experience in dealing with the Russians, experience in succoring freedoms in Europe, and experience in being victorious over an enemy.

President Truman knew the Cold War would come to be a major factor in defining his presidency when he bid an official farewell to the American public in 1953. In his farewell address, Truman told the American people, "I suppose history will remember my term in office as the years when the "cold war" began to overshadow our lives. I have had hardly a day in office that has not been dominated by this all-embracing struggle – this conflict between those who love freedom and those who would lead the world back into slavery and darkness. And always in the background there has been the atomic bomb."[1]

Even with his time in office being the start of the dangerous Cold War, Truman felt he had placed the United States on a path that would lead to its ultimate victory over communism. He clarified this point later in his farewell address stating, "But when history says that my term of office saw the beginning of the cold war, it will also say that in those 8 years we have set the course that can win it[2]…As the free world grows stronger, more united, and more attractive to men on both sides of the Iron Curtain – and as the Soviet hopes for easy expansion are blocked – then there will have to come a time of change in the Soviet world."[3] President Harry S. Truman had laid the foundation of the American response to the communist threat. It would be upon that foundation that victory would come to the United States and the free world in the Cold War.

---

1 Krugler, ed., *The Cold War*, 60.
2 Ibid.
3 Ibid., 61.

V

Dwight D. Eisenhower: No Equal

Occasionally world events seem to bring the right leader to the foreground at precisely the right time. Men and women with the necessary skillsets needed at a particular moment in history seem to sometimes appear as if they were a hero created by Hollywood. Heroes seem to step out on the stage as if they were written for a specific scene and were created to only meet the needs of the dangers found lurking in the plot. These individuals are few in numbers, but they are easily spotted through the prism of history even if their contemporaries miss their leading man status as their lives play out right in front of them, history seems to never miss out.

Dwight David Eisenhower was one of these characters. He almost appears destined to save the world from the tyranny of the Nazis and protect the western world from the onslaught of communism even though his rise to prominence looks as if was one of the most unlikely stories in the history of the world. He entered the world stage, compiled the necessary experience, won the adoration of millions of his fellow countrymen, became a hero to people all over the world, and kept the United States and the world safe from nuclear annihilation during his eight years as president of the United States.

Dwight D. Eisenhower came to the White House in 1953 after securing the first Republican presidential victory since Herbert Hoover's 1928 electoral triumph. There was more than just party politics that led people to cast their votes for him. With the Korean War dragging on with no end in sight, America turned to Eisenhower to guide them through the growing complexities of the Cold War. Soviet advances in atomic capabilities combined with communist aggression throughout the world increased the national desire to turn the keys of leadership to someone who had guided the nation through the toughest days of World War II.

As the tension with the Soviet Union reached new heights, Dwight D. Eisenhower offered the United States a qualified résumé unmatched by any of his contemporaries. It had become clear to Americans that Eisenhower's expertise on how to wage a successful war in Europe may again be needed. Simply put, there was no one better to deal with the Soviet threat than the man who had defeated Hitler and liberated Europe less than twenty years prior.

Before he became "Ike the General," Eisenhower had spent the majority of his adult life in military service. He had attended West Point beginning in 1911.[1] Eisenhower had only served state-side during World War I, but gained valuable experience in dealing with large numbers of troops. His actions as a leader at the World War I camp in Gettysburg led to a promotion to the rank of major in June of 1918.[2] Moving quickly up the ranks of military service, Eisenhower found himself tapped as the Supreme Commander of Allied Forces in the European Theater of World War II. He rose quickly from a colonel to the man who orchestrated the multinational D-Day invasion.[3] Being in charge of a worldwide coalition of freedom prepared Eisenhower with the skillset needed to be an effective president during the height of the Cold War.

The development of Dwight D. Eisenhower into the most qualified man to lead the free world as the Cold War intensified in the 1950s was largely based on his firsthand knowledge of Europe. Not only had Eisenhower orchestrated the D-Day invasion to liberate the continent from the Axis Powers in 1944, he had made a meticulous study of European battlefields from the First World War while stationed in Paris with General John

---

1 Evan Thomas, *Ike's Bluff: President Eisenhower's Secret Battle to Save the World* (New York: Little, Brown and Company, 2012), 403.

2 Jean Edward Smith, *Eisenhower in War and Peace* (New York: Random House Trade Paperbacks, 2013), 43.

3 Stephen E. Ambrose, *The Supreme Commander: The War Years of Dwight D. Eisenhower* (New York: Anchor Books, 2012), 319.

J. Pershing and the Battle Monuments Commission.[4] The result of Eisenhower's studies was the guidebook entitled, *A Guide to the American Battlefields of Europe*.[5] The experience also provided him with a deeper understanding of the geography of the continent.[6] This knowledge would give Eisenhower as a general the familiarity necessary to defeating Hitler during World War II, and Eisenhower the president the vision for potential conflict with the Soviet Union.

At the conclusion of World War II, Eisenhower had achieved a level of respect among the military and political leaders of the coalition he led to victory in Europe. This achievement played a significant role in his effectiveness during the Cold War. He had been an American who had liberated Europe from Fascism, but did so without alienating those he had liberated. He did view himself as American commander, but more importantly for his future role as the leader of the free world, he kept the appearance of never neglecting the concerns of the other nations of the Allies. Opinions of Eisenhower remained high throughout Great Britain and France after the war had concluded.[7]

After the conclusion of World War II, General Dwight D. Eisenhower received countless honors from foreign governments.

---

4 Smith, *Eisenhower in War and Peace*, 76
5 Ibid., 78.
6 Ibid., 79.
7 Ambrose, *The Supreme Commander*, 588.

The man who saved Europe was given the "Order of Merit" by Great Britain, the "Knight Gravel Cross of the Order of the Lion" by the Netherlands, "Knight of the Order of the Polonia Retetuta" by Poland, "Grand Officer of the Legion of Honor" by France, and the "Grand Cordon of the Order of Leopold" by Belgium.[8] Norway, Denmark, Luxembourg, Brazil, Chile, Ecuador, Haiti, Mexico, Panama, and other nations all decorated Eisenhower to express their gratitude for his role in the Allied victory.[9] Even the Soviet Union awarded him the "Order of Victory" and the "Order of Suvarov, First Class."[10] Few men in history have ever achieved the level of respect and honor that was bestowed on General Eisenhower in the aftermath of World War II.

When the Cold War began to heat up with war in Korea, Eisenhower was called upon by President Truman to put his uniform on again after a brief period as the president of Columbia University.[11] Truman tapped Eisenhower to head the newly formed NATO forces in Europe in 1950.[12] With the threat of communism rising, there was no man whose military prestige met that of Dwight Eisenhower. He was unanimously chosen by the members of NATO as the logical choice to lead the defense alliance and

---

8 Michael Korda, *Ike: An American Hero* (New York: Harper Collins, 2007). 592.
9 Ibid.
10 Ibid.
11 Smith, *Eisenhower in War and Peace*, 466-467.
12 Stephen E. Ambrose, *Eisenhower: Soldier and President* (New York: Simon and Schuster Paperbacks, 1990), 249.

to oversee the rearmament of Europe[13] Orchestrating one victory over a determined and dangerous foe just a few years earlier led to Eisenhower being called again for the potential defense of freedom in Europe.

President Harry S. Truman completely understood General Eisenhower's status as the most respected military leader in the Western world after World War II. In an unprecedented historical account, it has been reported that Truman even went as far as to offer Eisenhower the presidency in 1948.[14] Not knowing Eisenhower's true political party allegiance, Truman assessed the growing communist threat as his reelection neared and offered to serve only as vice-president if Eisenhower would be willing to accept the Democrat Party's nomination for president. Truman had already spoken highly of Eisenhower during the last days of World War II saying, "He's doing a whale of a job.... They are running him for president, which is ok with me. I'd turn it over to him now if I could."[15] Unfortunately for Truman and the Democrat Party, Eisenhower's secret political identity was actually leaning toward the Republican Party. This episode conveys the respect, admiration, and confidence in Eisenhower's leadership during the years following World War II. For a sitting president to be willing to give up his job to serve under another man proves

---

13 Ibid.
14 Nancy Gibbs and Michael Duffy, *The President's Club*, 61.
15 Ibid., 59.

that other man was no ordinary individual. Dwight Eisenhower was no ordinary individual on the world stage as the Cold War intensified around the globe.

Even though Eisenhower had spent the majority of his career outside the political arena, years of standing shoulder to shoulder with the great political leaders of the world seasoned him to take the reins of freedom as an American Cold War president. His rise to becoming one of the world's most trusted men whose opinions were highly sought had the outward appearance of being meteoric. Eisenhower had, however, put in many long hours and paid his dues as a student and active participant of world affairs. From the moment he stepped out onto the world stage at a press conference explaining Allied objective in the Mediterranean in 1942,[16] Ike became somewhat of a media sensation. His experience, aura, leadership skills, and welcoming smile helped Dwight D. Eisenhower take the steps toward leading the free world against the Soviet threat in 1950s.

---

16 Paul Johnson, *Eisenhower: A Life* (New York: Penguin Books, 2014), 28

VI

I shall go to Korea

The weight that the name of Dwight D. Eisenhower truly carried was put on display when he vowed to visit Korea while campaigning for president in 1952. About a month before Americans would go to the polls to select either Eisenhower or his democrat rival Adlai Stevenson, Eisenhower alleged President Truman had been unable to stop communism in Korea and other hot spots in the world.[1] Speaking to a crowd in Detroit, Eisenhower brought to the audience's mind the muscle he would bring to the White House if elected by saying, "I know something about the totalitarian mind."[2] Dwight Eisenhower knew how to defeat a hostile enemy and the American people trusted him to do it again.

---

1 Jim Newton, *Eisenhower: The White House Years* (New York: First Anchor Books, 2012.), 75.
2 Ibid.

He then vowed to personally travel to Korea and bring an end to the war by pledging, "I shall go to Korea."[3]

On Election Day 1952, the American people gave Dwight Eisenhower a resounding vote of confidence in his stature as not just a military leader, but a world leader. He easily won the election by receiving more votes than any other Republican candidate in history.[4] The ongoing Korean War was a large factor in Eisenhower's big victory. The American people were growing wary of slugging it out with the communist in Korea and wanted out of the war.[5] The fact that the United States relied on an almost completely draftee army[6] increased the desire to bring in a man with the credentials to bring the nation's young men home from a war that wasn't producing the resemblance of victory.

President Harry S. Truman's relationship with Dwight D. Eisenhower had become increasingly fractured over the war in Korea and other factors. Long gone were the days when Truman would happily turn over the executive branch to Eisenhower. After Eisenhower's victory, President Truman sent a telegraph to congratulate him on his big victory and his new status as president-elect. Still, Truman could not resist mocking Eisenhower's pledge to visit Korea in the telegram. He wrote to

---

3 Ibid.
4 Ibid., 76.
5 Smith, *Eisenhower in War and Peace*, 546-547.
6 Ibid., 546.

Eisenhower, "Congratulations on your overwhelming victory. The Independence (Truman's personal plane) will be at your disposal if you still desire to go to Korea."[7] The Democrats had viewed the pledge to visit Korea as grandstanding,[8] but Eisenhower fully intended to put the full force of his résumé to the battlegrounds and negotiating table of Korea.

In late November 1953, President-elect Eisenhower secretly left the United States to begin his journey to Korea.[9] Due to increasing danger throughout Korea and threats of assassination against the South Korean president, Eisenhower had to enter the peninsula under the strictest security and secrecy.[10] He would spend a total of three days in Korea assessing the situation and the terrain of the peninsula.[11] After visiting the battleground, Eisenhower was firmly convinced the war needed to end.[12] He later wrote after his trip to Korea concluded, "…we could not stand forever on as static front and continue to accept casualties without any visible results. Small attacks on small hills will not end this war."[13] Eisenhower would be inaugurated as president a month later.

As president-elect, Dwight Eisenhower realized the United

---

7   Ibid., 548.
8   Newton, *Eisenhower*, 76.
9   Ibid., 77.
10 Ibid., 77-78.
11 Smith, *Eisenhower in War and Peace*, 557-558.
12 Ibid., 560.
13 Ibid., 559-560.

States could not afford to continuously fight wars like Korea. Possibly due to his military background and firsthand knowledge of the burdens of sending young men to die, he came to denounce "limited wars" like Korea.[14] As president, Eisenhower wanted to keep the United States out of "brushfire wars."[15] Bringing the United States out of the limited war of the Truman era meant an overhaul to the way America was meeting the communist threat. One of the top priorities of the Eisenhower administration was fulfilling the pledge of ending the war in Korea.[16] Also, he realized he could set the stage for the larger Cold War chess match by sending a message on *how* he ended that war.

By the time Eisenhower had entered office, most Americans had been psychologically effected by the Cold War in some way. Hysteria over the atomic bomb had gripped the American public.[17] The views on atomic weapons were about to change from within the White House. Eisenhower quickly came to the realization during the early days of his presidency that America's atomic arsenal could not only provide the leverage for bringing the Korean War to an end, but for checking all current and future communist aggression around the globe.

---

14 John Lewis Gaddis, *The Cold War*, 61.
15 John Lewis Gaddis, *Strategies of Containment: A Critical Appraisal of American National Security during the Cold War* (New York: Oxford University Press, 2005), 165
16 Newton, *Eisenhower*, 101.
17 Thomas, *Ike's Bluff*, 72.

As he attempted to orchestrate an end to the Korean conflict, Eisenhower was looking into nuclear options for the Korean peninsula.[18] He had asked his military advisor to look into ways that nuclear weapons could be used in the conflict to precipitate an honorable end to the fighting.[19] Eisenhower allowed his administration to advance the idea that nuclear attacks were being prepared in order to bluff the Chinese and North Koreans into ending the war.[20]

Another momentous event on the Cold War landscape came with the death of Joseph Stalin on March 5, 1953.[21] The Soviet leader's death occurred just two months after Eisenhower came to office[22] and provided the new American president an opening for potential negotiations to end the conflict in Korea. There was one major problem with the death of Stalin and that was the fact that America had no plan for the event.[23] There had been much talk about the impact of the Soviet leader's death over the years, but there was no concrete plan on how to respond or what might happen in the Soviet Union now that he had died.[24] In spite of all the uncertainty, Stalin's death did bring about a potential for

---

18 Gaddis, *The Cold War*, 63.
19 Ibid.
20 Ibid.
21 Thomas, *Ike's Bluff*, 74.
22 Gaddis, *The Cold War*, 63.
23 Ambrose, *Eisenhower*, 311.
24 Ibid.

peace. Whereas Stalin relished the ongoing conflict in Korea as a means to exhaust the West in manpower, courage, and materials; the new leadership was eager to see the war come to a close.[25]

A little more than month after the death of Joseph Stalin, Eisenhower delivered a speech that embodied his desire to make more than just an armistice in Korea, but a lasting peace in the Cold War. The speech was to be delivered to the American Society of Newspaper Editors in Washington's Statler Hotel.[26] In the speech that would become known as "A Chance for Peace," Eisenhower broadened his hopes of peace by setting forth a Cold War peace plan.[27] He claimed that he needed to put forth a peace plan before he verbally attacked Russia's record of aggression any farther.[28]

The night before Eisenhower was to deliver the important speech, he was hit with a severe intestinal ailment and excruciating pain.[29] At one point during the speech, he began sweating and feeling so dizzy that he had to grip the podium tightly to steady him.[30] He soldiered through his speech telling the audience that the Soviet Union leadership had an opportunity to help

---

25 Thomas, *Ike's Bluff*, 74.
26 Ambrose, *Eisenhower*, 324.
27 David A Nichols, *Ike and McCarthy: Dwight Eisenhower's Secret Campaign against Joseph McCarthy* (New York: Simon and Schuster, 2017), 34-35.
28 Ibid. 35.
29 Smith, *Eisenhower in War and Peace*, 575.
30 Ambrose, *Eisenhower*, 325.

change the direction of the world from constant fear of war to a path of peace.[31] He believed the Soviets needed to be a part of the unification of Germany and spreading of freedom among communist nations in Eastern Europe.[32] Eisenhower spoke about the different paths of the United States and Soviet Union, but he mentioned how reconciliation and peace could be attained by saying, "The first great step along this way must be the conclusion of an honorable armistice in Korea."[33] Challenging the Soviet Union again on the ongoing situation in Korea, Eisenhower said, "Is the new leadership of the Soviet Union prepared to use its decisive influence in the Communist world, including control of the flow of arms, to bring not merely an expedient truce in Korea but genuine peace in Asia?"[34]

Arguably, the speech is considered the best oratory moment that President Dwight D. Eisenhower had during his time in office. The speech was praised by the American and foreign press.[35] Not only did the speech shed light on how to move forward in Korea, but the speech spoke on the overall issues of war, peace, economics, foreign relations, Cold War disarmament, and human decency. Eisenhower made finding a solution to the

---

31 Smith, *Eisenhower in War and Peace*, 575.
32 Ambrose, *Eisenhower*, 325.
33 "Chance for Peace Speech." Accessed July 10, 2017. https://www.eisenhower.archives.gov.
34 Ibid.
35 Ambrose, *Eisenhower*, 326.

overall complexities of the Cold War a priority with passages such as: "Every gun that is made, every warship launched, every rocket fired signifies, in the final sense, a theft from those who hunger and are not fed, those who are cold and are not clothed. This world in arms is not spending money alone. It is spending the sweat of its laborers, the genius of its scientists, the hopes of its children. The cost of one modern heavy bomber is this: a modern brick school in more than 30 cities. It is two electric power plants, each serving a town of 60,000 population. It is two fine, fully equipped hospitals. It is some 50 miles of concrete highway. We pay for a single fighter plane with a half million bushels of wheat. We pay for a single destroyer with new homes that could have housed more than 8,000 people. This, I repeat, is the best way of life to be found on the road the world has been taking. This is not a way of life at all, in any true sense. Under the cloud of threatening war, it is humanity hanging from a cross of iron."[36]

As he looked for ways to end the conflict in Korea, Eisenhower realized pressure must be applied to the Chinese to bring it to a satisfactory conclusion.[37] Against the wishes of some key allies, Eisenhower allowed the United States to give the impression of willingness to go nuclear on the peninsula. He let the Chinese leadership know through subtle messages that he was willing to

---

36 "Chance for Peace Speech." Accessed July 10, 2017. https://www.eisenhower.archives.gov.
37 Ambrose, *Eisenhower*, 303.

use all weapons in America's arsenal if they didn't cooperate with the peace negotiations.[38] More than anything, his reputation as the general who had already used everything in the American arsenal to defeat Hitler allowed his nuclear threat to be taken seriously. No one else's words could have carried the weight of Dwight D. Eisenhower.[39]

On July 27, 1953 (Korean time-It was still July 26, 1953 in the United States) the Korean War came to a close.[40] All the major participants signed an armistice essentially ending the conflict. Over 140,000 Americans had been killed, injured, or reported missing during the struggle.[41] The exact number of casualties stood at 142,091.[42] A high price had been paid for containing communism. It was a price that Eisenhower believed could be avoided in the future by properly advancing American nuclear capabilities and expertly bluffing the willingness of the United States to use them. Due to Dwight D. Eisenhower's nuclear threat and the prestige of his name, he was able to remove the United States from the first full-scale combat of the Cold War.

---

38   Ibid.
39   Ibid.
40   Smith, *Eisenhower in War and Peace*, 577.
41   Ibid.
42   Ibid.

VII

Calming the McCarthy Storm

During the early days of the Eisenhower administration, Senator Joseph McCarthy continued to grab headlines with his sensational claims of communist agents and sympathizers infiltrating the United States government. Dwight D. Eisenhower faced an interesting dilemma as the new president of the United States. McCarthy was a member of the same political party as Eisenhower and even though the president disapproved of the Senator's tactics, there was no denying he held power in Washington. Direct conflict with Senator McCarthy could be potentially damaging in the political climate of the early 1950s.

President Eisenhower had failed on the campaign trail in 1952 by not directly attacking McCarthy on behalf of his friend, General George C. Marshall. McCarthy claimed that the highly respected general, and member of the Truman administration, was less than loyal to the United States in the Cold War struggle.

Eisenhower had prepared to come to the aid with a public address in McCarthy's home state of Wisconsin. At the last minute, Eisenhower left the passage about Marshall out of his speech. When a draft of the speech containing the Marshall passage was picked up by the press, Eisenhower looked as if he had backed down to the scare tactics of Senator McCarthy.[1]

Now that Eisenhower was in the White House and the undisputed leader of his political party, he decided it was time to alienate McCarthy from the mainstream political climate of the day. Eisenhower would not follow Truman's example of openly attacking McCarthy, but would kill McCarthy with silence. The president had decided to never mention the senator by name saying, "I had made up my mind how I was going to handle McCarthy. This was to ignore him… I would give him no satisfaction. I'd never defend anything. I don't care what he called me, or mentioned, or put in the papers, I'd just ignore him."[2] Eisenhower also said of McCarthy, "Nothing will be so effective in combatting his particular kind trouble-making as to ignore him. This he cannot stand."[3]

Eisenhower had his strategy against McCarthy in place. McCarthy represented the worst of American Cold War fears and the president wanted to shine light on the wrongness of

---

1 Nichols, *Ike and McCarthy*, 57.
2 Jon Meacham, *The Soul of America: The Battle for our Better Angels* (New York: Random House, 2018), 198
3 Nichols, *Ike and McCarthy*, 10.

his actions by not giving his name any publicity in the press. The president followed this path when he indirectly rebuked McCarthy's purging of American overseas libraries from material he deemed pro-communist. Speaking at the Dartmouth College commencement ceremony in 1953, President Eisenhower stated, "Don't join the book burners. Don't think you are going to conceal faults by concealing evidence that they ever existed. Don't be afraid to go into your library and read every book, as long as that document does not offend your own ideas of decency. That should be the only censorship. How will we defeat communism unless we know what it is, and what it teaches, and why does it have such appeal for men, why are so many people swearing allegiance to it."[4] Eisenhower was afraid America would lose itself in its fight against communism if the majority of its citizens followed the McCarthy path.

Eisenhower's refusal to acknowledge McCarthy had the desired effect. More and more news agencies and members of the U.S. government began to realize the poisoning influence of McCarthy's form of anti-communist crusading. Although he remained a popular political figure, McCarthy would overplay his popularity by attacking the U.S. Army. During televised hearings into that branch of the military, Senator Joe McCarthy's reign of terror unraveled when his questioning of the loyalty of a member

---

4   Meacham, *The Soul of America*, 198-199

of Army's legal team backfired in 1954. The counsel for the Army, Joseph N. Welch, reached a point of frustration with McCarthy's witch hunt causing him to exclaim, "You have done enough. Have you no sense of decency, sir, at long last? Have you left no sense of decency?"[5]

After his exchange with Welch, McCarthy's days as a prominent political player were numbered. He was censured by his colleagues in the Senate and began to increase his already dangerous consumption of alcohol. Joseph McCarthy would die three years after his political power unraveled in 1957.[6] His legacy is one of power misused and a constitution unnecessarily endangered by the real threat of the Cold War, while Eisenhower is remembered as a statesman worthy praise for his handling of McCarthy. The president of the United States defended the basic principles of the constitution from a demagogue while maintaining the necessary footing in the fight against communism.

---

5   Ibid., 201.
6   Ibid., 205.

VIII

Trouble in Vietnam

Asia would provide another Cold War hotspot in the fall of 1954 when France lost its colony of Vietnam in humiliating fashion.[1] After the French forces were defeated at Dien Bien Phu in May of 1954, the country of Vietnam was divided into two nations at a peace conference in Geneva, Switzerland.[2] The communist took control the north, and the south became a fragile democracy.[3] The stability of the democratic government in the south was a source of concern for those who wished to see communism contained.[4] With the division of Vietnam, the Cold War landscape had been altered again and the United States had to decide what role it would take in the Cold War affairs of Asia.

---

1   Thomas, *Ike's Bluff*, 130.
2   Ibid.
3   Ibid
4   Ibid.

The fall of Vietnam came at a crossroads of world history. The United States had no real desire to aid colonial powers in their centuries-old struggle to force their will over smaller nations in less affluent areas of the world.[5] On the other hand, the United States also had zero interest in destroying the necessary alliances with European colonial powers needed to provide economic and military stability to the European continent.[6] Even without the United States directly supporting European colonialism, America became the symbol of colonial aggression through the actions of their allies.[7] The United States was slowly becoming guilty by association in the eyes of many residents living in underdeveloped nations.

Much like the conflict in Korea, Stalin had urged the Vietnamese to fight against the French.[8] Stalin did not try a full-scale attempt to exert Soviet influence on Vietnam, but he did urge Ho Chi Minh to destroy the French forces in Asia.[9] This era of the Cold War provided one of the few instances when American/Soviet foreign policies came into agreement. Both nations were in opposition to European colonialism as the 1950s began. The only difference was the fact that the United States was tied too closely

---

5   Gaddis, *The Cold War*, 122
6   Ibid., 123.
7   Ibid.
8   Ibid., 122
9   Ibid.

to its European allies to portray a substantial separation from the practices of colonialism.[10]

Vietnam would confront President Eisenhower with another important decision. He would have to find an adequate response to the fall of the nation to the communist sphere that would promote American interest in lives, material, and global prestige. Vietnam would be one of the few pieces of ground lost to communism during the Eisenhower presidency; even if much of the nation was already under the control of Ho Chi Minh when he entered the White House.[11] Even as Eisenhower would grow concerned over comparisons to Truman's loss of China, he became dedicated to keeping the United States out of a ground war in Vietnam.

From the start, President Eisenhower had been critical of the French battle plan that led to their demise, as well as voicing criticism toward France's unwillingness to grant independence to Vietnam.[12] Even with his concerns about the situation in Vietnam, Eisenhower still understood the Cold War ramifications of the conflict. He responded with limitations to a French request for twenty-five bombers to assist in the Dien Bien Phu battle by sending only ten bombers for the French to use against the Vietnamese.[13] Eisenhower was extremely cautious not to implicate the United

---

10   Ibid., 122-123.
11   Gaddis, *Strategies of Containment*, 162.
12   Smith, *Eisenhower in War and Peace*, 609.
13   Ibid., 610.

States in another ground war in Asia, but many Americans alertly realized the similarities to the war in Korea. More and more members of Congress expressed concern about being drug into another Korea-style war as the French were nearing defeat in Vietnam.[14] Eisenhower knew the dangers of throwing American forces into the harsh terrain of Vietnam. As only a general could, he analyzed the battlefield and became convinced Vietnam was a place ripe with potentials for disaster. Eisenhower remarked that the jungles of Vietnam would "absorb our troops by the divisions!"[15]

The true test for Eisenhower in Vietnam was to find a way to halt the spread of communism without exhausting American lives and morale in the process. In the other side of the Cold War chessboard was the new Soviet leader Nikita Khrushchev who now controlled the direction of the communist world. Khrushchev was more willing to become directly involved in the affairs of developing nations than Stalin had been as the Soviet leader.[16] Khrushchev believed he could find an opening with nations who were throwing off the shackles of colonialism and bring them into the communist camp.[17]

It was under this cloud that Eisenhower delivered the famous "Domino Theory" concept.[18] A month before the final French defeat

---

14   Ibid.
15   Thomas, *Ike's Bluff*, 120.
16   Gaddis, *The Cold War*, 122-123
17   Ibid.
18   Ibid., 123.

in Vietnam, Eisenhower spoke at a news conference about dominoes in context of the Cold War.[19] He spoke to the reporters saying, "You have a row of dominoes set up, you knock over the first one, and what will happen to the last one is certainty that it will go over very quickly."[20] Eisenhower also stated, "the possible consequences of the loss [of Indochina] are just incalculable to the free world."[21]

Eisenhower came to the realization during while watching the unfolding crisis in Vietnam that the jungles of Vietnam were not the place to commit U.S. forces to another Korean-style war. When many members of his administration began to look to nuclear weapons as a means to assisting the French, Eisenhower exercised restraint stating, "We can't use those awful things against Asians for the second time in less than ten years. My God."[22] Eisenhower was willing to fight in Vietnam to stop communism, but he assessed the current situation as impossible for victory. The old military man refused to commit his troops to an unwinnable war[23] even if that meant allowing communism to gain a foothold in Southeast Asia.

---

19 Smith, *Eisenhower in War and Peace*, 611.
20 Ibid.
21 Jeffrey Frank, *Ike and Dick: Portrait of a Strange Political Marriage* (New York: Simon and Schuster Paperbacks, 2013), 90.
22 Thomas, *Ike's Bluff*, 129.
23 Ibid., 130-133.

IX

New Look

If President Eisenhower was not willing to become bogged down in brushfire wars like the one presented in Vietnam, yet willing to rely on nuclear weapons as peace-keeping weapon, what was the essence of his approach to the problems of the Cold War? How would Eisenhower stop the spread of communism around the globe? Eisenhower's approach to communism became known as the "New Look" since it was a new approach to America's defense policy.[1] Under Eisenhower's leadership, the United States would reduce the size of the traditional military and rely more on the deterrence provided by nuclear weapons.[2] The United States would try to keep the peace by flexing its atomic muscle rather than jump into brushfire wars to achieve containment.[3] "The New

---

1   Smith, *Eisenhower in War and Peace*, 643.
2   Ibid.
3   Ibid.

Look" approach would give the United States "more bang for its buck."[4]

Cold War historian John Lewis Gaddis summarized the "New Look" strategy by saying it provided "maximum possible deterrence of communism at the minimum possible cost."[5] Eisenhower would use nuclear weapons to deter communist aggression around the globe.[6] The United States had already seen some results to this approach through Eisenhower's handling of the armistice in Korea. The new nuclear-based approach was also referred to as "massive retaliation" for promising to bring nuclear weapons into almost any Cold War hotspot.[7] The "New Look" was about to be put to almost continual tests as the Cold War moved deeper into the 1950s.

Altering paths from his predecessor, Eisenhower was not fully committed to simple containment. He was willing to investigate ways to "roll back" communism and give the Soviets a challenge in different parts of the globe.[8] This would be the piece of the "New Look" that was not fully under the spell of atomic weapons. Eisenhower had also fell in love with covert operations.

The Eisenhower administration tackled communism head-on by staging coups in various parts of the world. The year 1953 saw

---

4   Ibid.
5   Gaddis, *Strategies of Containment*, 162.
6   Ibid.
7   Smith, *Eisenhower in War and Peace*, 643.
8   Newton, *Eisenhower*, 162.

the culmination of work between the United States and Great Britain with the arrest and removal of the Iranian prime minister who was flirting too close for comfort with the communist sphere.[9] Led by the grandson of Theodore Roosevelt, the U.S. secret operation brought the pro-American Iranian shah back into power.[10] Thwarting potential communist allies gave Eisenhower strong sense of trust in the Central Intelligence Agency and its ability to led successful covert operations.[11] The C.I.A. would increase in importance as the Cold War moved forward.

---

9   Geoffrey Perret, *Eisenhower* (Holbrook: Adams Media Corporation, 1999). 478-479.
10 Ibid.
11 Ibid.

X

Suez Crisis

As the United States moved into an election year in 1956, the post-Stalin Soviet Union began to look for ways to exert its influence in new parts of the world. In response, President Eisenhower began to realize the necessity of attempting to persuade nations like Egypt into joining the pro-American camp of the Cold War. Particular interest was put on Egyptian leader Gamal Abdul Nasser and his influence in the Middle East. Nasser was on the verge of purchasing weapons from the communist bloc and aligning his nation with American opposition. This turn of events would signal a significant diplomacy defeat for the United States in the Cold War chess game in the Middle East Theater. The U.S. was open to ways to block potential Soviet courting of Egypt and its leader.[1]

---

1   John Lewis Gaddis, *We Now Know: Rethinking Cold War History* (Oxford: Oxford University Press, 1997), 171.

By 1956, the Soviet Union had another monumental opportunity to establish a Middle Eastern foothold by potentially funding Nasser's Anwar Dam project on the Nile River.[2] The United States was fully aware of the possibility of Soviet involvement in the project and realized it would be able to block Soviet intentions by funding the dam with American dollars. The U.S. had reached out to the Egyptians in regard to potentially funding the project, but the relationship between the United States and Egypt was beginning to wear thin as the dam project neared fruition. Egypt would never receive U.S. assistance in the Anwar Dam Project setting off a chain of events that almost ended in the eruption of the third world war.

The reasons for U.S. funds for the dam falling through were based on the United States losing patients with Nasser and his actions. To the annoyance of the United States, Nasser had violated the Baghdad Pact, recognized the People's Republic of China as a sovereign nation, and invited the Soviet Union into the affairs of the Middle East. These actions caused the United States to cool on its desire to assist Egypt in the Anwar Dam Project creating a rift between the two nations.[3]

The man who finally broke the news to the Egyptians that they would not be receiving any U.S. assistance on the dam was

---

2   Ibid.
3   Ibid.

Secretary of State John Foster Dulles. Nasser and the Egyptians were informed by the Secretary on July 19, 1956 and told they may need to either scrap the dam completely, or look elsewhere for the funds. Nasser responded by announcing the nationalizing the Suez Canal on July 26, 1956[4] in a dramatic speech. Speaking for approximately three hours in Alexandria and filling every possible sentence with anti-American rhetoric, Nasser solidified his new stance as a potential foe to the United States.[5]

At first, most people in world would have been forgiven if they missed this action as a potential moment of crisis in the Cold War. While being on the president's radar, Nasser's move did not fully attract Eisenhower's attention. Nasser believed the nationalization of the Suez Canal would be a source of revenue for Egypt that could pay for the dam and replace the money they would now not be receiving from the United States.[6] Arguably, the decision to nationalize the Suez Canal hurt Great Britain most of all while not being the most important event in the opinion of American foreign affairs. British troops, ships, and oil supplies all came through the canal with regularity. Great Britain and France even

---

4   Ibid.
5   David A. Nichols, *Eisenhower 1956: The President's Year of Crisis, Suez and the Brink of War* (New York: Simon and Schuster Paperbacks, 2011), 131.
6   Ibid.

had economic interest in the company that operated the canal, the Suez Canal Company.⁷

With such interest at stake for the British, it could not have come as a surprise to President Eisenhower when news of the British and French planning to wage war on Egypt was brought to his attention. The traditional American allies were considering invading Egypt and retaking the canal. News of a potential war created a tense world for Eisenhower to navigate as his reelection campaign was gearing up for the final push to keep him in the White House. To the president's delight however, both nations appeared to scrap their plans for war after Eisenhower announced he believed Egypt was within its legal right to nationalize the canal since every foot of the canal was within Egyptian territory.⁸ Peace appeared to be even more likely after Eisenhower refused to support a military approach to the situation and Britain and France indicated that any attempt to retake the canal was now officially shelved.⁹

As summer began to fade into fall in 1956, the prospect of war in the Middle East seemed to disappear with the warm temperatures. The calm was welcomed by President Eisenhower since he had to deal with not just foreign and domestic challenges over the past few years, but he had to personally battle health issues that reappeared in the midst of the crisis in the Suez. In 1955,

---

7 Ibid., 133-134.
8 Smith, *Eisenhower in War and Peace*, 694.
9 Ibid., 694-695.

Eisenhower had suffered a heart attack that forced him to stay in the hospital for six weeks before returning to his Gettysburg, Pennsylvania farm to recuperate.[10] It was during the Suez Crisis and his reelection campaign in 1956 that Eisenhower had another health scare when he suffered from a severe attack of ileitis in August.[11] An unexpected turn in the Suez crisis would soon take away any chance the president would have to rest after his illness.

Luckily, President Eisenhower quickly recovered from his health scare and was ready for the Republican convention in late August. He had briefly flirted with the idea of not seeking a second term after his heart attack the previous year but realized the world needed his continued leadership. After being cleared by doctors to run for a second term, Eisenhower threw his hat in the ring for another election.

As his campaign fired up, British Prime Minister Anthony Eden told the president that the British were moving completely away from military intervention in Egypt.[12] In reality, Eden had misled the president. Great Britain and France were actually preparing for a war with the help of their new ally Israel.[13] The calm in the Suez that Eisenhower was currently enjoying was not

---

10 Johnson, *Eisenhower*, 103-104.
11 Ibid., 105.
12 Smith, *Eisenhower*, 696.
13 Ibid.

the beginning of a lasting peace, but the calm before a much larger storm with potential global implications.

Behind Eisenhower's back, the French, British, and Israelis were hatching an elaborate plan to end the nationalization of the Suez Canal. Not only were the nations preparing to retake the canal, but they were intent on removing Nasser from power as well. The French had grown close to Israel and sent the Israelis weapons even before the Suez Crisis.[14] Together, France and Israel approached Britain with a plan for ending Nasser's control of the canal that included:

1. Israel attacking Egypt
2. The British and French would move into Egypt to protect shipping in the Suez Canal
3. Then, Great Britain and France would demand an end to the Israel/Egypt hostilities and demand both sides move at least 10 miles away from the canal.
4. Israel would then agree to the demands while it was expected that Nasser would not.
5. British and French ground forces move in, retake the canal completely, and topple Nasser.[15]

---

14 Michael Doran, *Ike's Gamble: America's Rise to Dominance in the Middle East* (New York: Free Press, 20160, 188.
15 Ibid., 189.

With few modifications to the plan, Great Britain agreed to the proposal on October 23, 1956. A few days later on October 29th, Israeli forces moved into Egypt to begin executing the plan with Britain and France.[16] President Eisenhower felt completely betrayed by his allies when he learned of Israel's attack on Egypt.[17] Feeling mislead by his allies and realizing he needed to live up to an earlier agreement the United States had signed pledging the nation to protect any other nation attacked in the Middle East, Eisenhower had his Secretary of State inform Israel that they may be facing sanctions for their actions in Egypt.[18]

With the situation growing more dangerous with each passing day, Eisenhower was at odds with his traditional allies. He even stated during the crisis that the United States "cannot be bound by our traditional alliances."[19] It was becoming increasingly clear to Eisenhower that the traditional powers of Europe were fading and their handling of the Suez Crisis illustrated they were no longer able to maintain their previous positions as colonial powers in a changing world.[20] Eisenhower had admired the fighting spirit of Great Britain[21] in the past, but now he was perplexed and angry at how badly they had handled events in Egypt. As president, he

---

16 Smith, *Eisenhower*, 697.
17 Ibid.
18 Nichols, *Eisenhower 1956*, 203.
19 Doran, *Ike's Gamble*, 193.
20 Ibid., 194-196.
21 Johnson, *Eisenhower*, 106-107.

now feared that the nation's old allies could drag the U.S. down with them if he was not careful.[22]

Eisenhower made the difficult and shocking decision to go against traditional American allies during the Suez Crisis. Shocking to the world, but not to anyone who knew Dwight D. Eisenhower, he decided to support Egypt over Great Britain, France, and Israel. Citing the Tripartite Declaration of 1950 which the U.S. signed, Eisenhower announced the U.S. position. The Tripartite Declaration stated that the United States, Great Britain, and France would support any victim of aggression in the Middle East.[23] This previous agreement made it clear to President Eisenhower that the U.S must stand with Egypt and that the British and French were definitely on the wrong side of the crisis. After hitting the British with financial pressure[24], the United States was eventually able to bring the turmoil in Egypt to close without the intervention of the Soviet Union and a costly war.

By bringing up the previous agreement over the protection of Middle East, Eisenhower showed the steps he was willing to take to maintain peace and American honor. His stance on the Suez Crisis illustrated the U.S. had definitely emerged from World War II as the most powerful and influential nation in the Western Alliance. Even at the expense of traditional allies, President

---

22 Doran, *Ike's Gamble*, 194-196.
23 Nichols, *Eisenhower 1956*, 203-204
24 Smith, *Eisenhower in War and Peace*, 702-704.

Dwight D. Eisenhower made it clear that he was dedicated to keeping peace, that he could not be bullied, and that he was a man of his word. He called out allies who were wrong and stood with an unexpected nation to bring stability to an unstable situation.

Part III

1957-1960

"In the councils of government, we must guard against the acquisition of unwarranted influence, whether sought or unsought, by the military-industrial complex."
-President Dwight D. Eisenhower

I

Sputnik

The Cold War seemed to continuously reach new locations on the map during the first decade of its existence. Spreading from disagreements over post-war Europe into armed conflict in Asia, to the Middle East, and into Latin America. Seemingly, no part of the world was untouched from the grip Cold War politics. In the late 1950s, the rivalry between the United States and the Soviet Union reached newer and more breathtaking settings than ever before when it left the boundaries of earth and moved into a space race between the two nations.

The origins of the space race lay in desire of both nations to become the first to put an artificial satellite into orbit. The United States had been trying to develop satellites to orbit the earth as far back as 1955 but had not finished the technology when the Soviet Union surprisingly beat the U.S. into space. The Soviets achieved worldwide acclaim on October 4, 1957 when they successfully launched the small but effective Sputnik I. No more than the size of a beach ball, Sputnik I orbited the earth at a size bigger than the satellite being developed in the United States.[1]

As Sputnik I orbited the earth, the American public was not only embarrassed by being beaten into space by the remarkable Soviet achievement, but fear gripped the U.S. as the possibility of the Soviet Union being close to the development of placing atomic weapons on satellites or ballistic missiles looked to be a reality.[2] The United States began almost immediately to attempt to make up the lost ground to the Soviet Union. Another remarkable achievement by Soviet scientist rocked the world later in the same year when Sputnik II was launched.[3] The United States needed to regain its footing in the Cold War battlefront of math and science.

It became apparent to the U.S. government that something must be done to counter the Soviet achievements in space technology. The initial reaction of the U.S. government spelled out the fears created by Sputnik in an evaluation of the matter which stated, "American prestige is viewed as having sustained a severe blow…The satellite is, of course, most widely and readily accepted as proof of the scientific and technical leadership by

---

1   NASA. Accessed March 24, 2018. https://history.nasa.gov/sputnik/.
2   Ibid.
3   Ibid.

those with the least scientific and political sophistication."[4] The U.S. had to regain the trust of the average citizen of the world to maintain its accepted position as the world leader in science and technology.

The National Science Board responded to the concern caused by Sputnik by issuing a statement that read, "We recognize that our nation's future rests in major degree upon the soundness of our system of education and our people's respect for scientific endeavor, based upon an understanding of its importance in the modern world."[5] With this in mind, the United States government created the National Aeronautics and Space Administration with the National Aeronautics and Space Act in 1958.[6] The government also insisted that increased emphasis on math and science in the American educational system become the new norm.

The Cold War had now turned into a space race that would continue for the next decade and at some degree for the duration of the Cold War. The United States was taken off-guard by the success of Sputnik and the abilities of the Soviet scientists, but

---

4   "Reaction to the Soviet Satellite - A Preliminary Evaluation." Dwight D. Eisenhower Presidential Library, Museum and Boyhood Home. Accessed March 24, 2018. https://www.eisenhower.archives.gov/research/online_documents/sputnik.html

5   "Statement by the National Science Board in Response to Russian Satellite, October 1957." Dwight D. Eisenhower Presidential Library, Museum and Boyhood Home. Accessed March 24, 2018. https://www.eisenhower.archives.gov/research/online_documents/sputnik.html

6   NASA. Accessed March 24, 2018. https://history.nasa.gov/sputnik/.

the American government dug in its heels to meet the Soviets head-on. The result of Sputnik was the birth of the space race and further proof that the United States and the Soviet Union were operating in different sphere of influence that now made space exploration a necessity.

II

The Kitchen Debate 1959

Vice-president Richard Nixon had proven himself to be of value to the Eisenhower administration on more than one occasion. He was often asked to be the face of the United States around the world in visits to friendly, as well as potentially hostile, nations. Nixon had impressed his peers with the way he helped steer the ship of state through Eisenhower's health scares and the manner in which he conducted himself when traveling abroad as the representative of the United States.

In 1959, Nixon traveled to the heart of American Cold War opposition by visiting the Soviet Union. The United States and the Soviet Union had decided to allow the citizens of both nations to see how the other side lived. The Cold War foes decided to host exhibitions that would highlight the technological advancements and the daily lives of citizens of each nation. The Soviets would hold an exhibit on Soviet life in New York and the United States would do the same in Moscow in 1959. Vice-president Nixon was dispatched by the Eisenhower administration to represent the U.S. at the opening of the American exhibit in Moscow. This meant Richard Nixon would also be coming face-to-face with Nikita Khrushchev.[1]

Upon arriving in Moscow and touring the American exhibition with Khrushchev and a group of reporters from both nations, the Soviet leader proved to be his usual combative self. He verbally assaulted Nixon, the United States, and capitalism at every chance. He mocked the advances made by the United States as he witnessed a demonstration of American television technology in the exhibit.[2] Khrushchev had come to fight and he was hitting Nixon with all the anti-capitalism greatest hits of the Soviet propaganda machine. Like everything else during the Cold War, there was no such thing as a casual meeting between any representatives of the two opposing nations. This was never truer than on this occasion.

Khrushchev had started his taunting of the United States by asking how long the U.S. had existed. When the answer came back that the U.S. had been around for 150 years, Khrushchev answered in his usual arrogant bravado saying, "Then we'll say America had existed for 150 years and here is its level. We have

---

1   John A. Farrell, *Richard Nixon: A Life* (New York: Doubleday, 2017), 269.
2   Ibid., 270.

existed almost 42 years and in another 7 years we will be on the same level as America. And then we'll move ahead. When we pass you along the way we'll greet you amicably like this. [Khrushchev waves his hand.] Then if you like, we can stop and invite you to catch up."[3] Statements such as this were more than the communist-hating Nixon could bear.

The debate turned to the availability of information and the state of a free press in both nations. As the two men battled the virtues of capitalism/democracy and communism, Khrushchev attacked the fairness of the American press stating, "…The camera is yours, you speak English and I am speaking Russian. Your English words are being taped and will be shown and heard, but what I am saying is being interpreted only in your ear, and therefore the American people won't hear what I have said. These are unequal conditions!"[4]

Nixon responded by educating Khrushchev on the fairness and freedom of the press in the United States. "…I can assure you that you never make a statement here that you don't think we read in the United States…Every word that you have said has been taken down, and I will promise you that every word that you have said

---

3   David Krugler, ed., *The Cold War: Core Documents* (Ashland: Ashbrook Center, 2018), 74.

4   Ibid, 76.

here will be reported in the United States and they will see you on television.,"⁵ responded Nixon.

As Nixon and Khrushchev moved into the next portion of the exhibit, Nixon had reached his limit and was now bracing to fight back. The two men squared off in a debate over the central themes of the Cold War. Becoming known as the "kitchen debate" since the heated discussion took place in a model of the modern American kitchen, Nixon stood up to the Soviet leader showing Khrushchev that he was no pushover.⁶ Nixon stood his ground with finger pointing, posturing, and a heated defense of the American way of life and system of government. ⁷

Khrushchev and Nixon later turned the focus of their impromptu debate toward the lives of the average citizen in both nations. When Khrushchev made a statement about the model American kitchen being no different from the technology available to Soviet citizens, Nixon responded by saying, "This is the newest model. This is the kind which is built in thousands of units for direct installation in houses…Let me give you an example…any steel worker could buy this house. They earn $3 an hour. This

---

5   Ibid.
6   Evan Thomas, *Being Nixon: A Man Divided* (New York: Random House, 2016), 105.
7   Ibid.

house costs about $100 a month to buy on a contract running twenty-five to thirty years."[8]

The press gave Nixon very favorable reviews of his exchange with Nikita Khrushchev. Nixon later recalled the event in his memoirs as being "widely reported."[9] The "kitchen debate" portion of the exchange created a sensation around the globe. Although not televised like the earlier portions of the Nixon/Khrushchev debate, the portion occurring in the model kitchen was printed in newspapers throughout the United States accompanied by pictures of Nixon pointing directly into Khrushchev's chest.[10] Nixon appeared strong against the attack of the Soviet leader and gained praise throughout the west as defender of the free world, capitalism, democracy, the Eisenhower administration, and the United States.

---

8   Krugler, ed., The Cold War, 77.
9   Richard Nixon, *RN: The Memoirs of Richard Nixon* (New York: Grossett & Dunlap, 1978), 209.
10 Ibid.

III

U-2, Spies, and Open Skies

Due to Eisenhower's unshakable confidence in the New Look being the direction the United States needed to take in preparation for Cold War retaliation, the Strategic Air Command became increasingly important.[1] The Strategic Air Command would be the means through which the U.S. could deliver weapons of mass destruction to the communist's doorstep. Eisenhower stated in 1957 that the United States needed to put every available resource into the development of the Strategic Air Command and hydrogen bombs after learning an estimated 50 million Americans could perish in a nuclear attack.[2] The problem facing Strategic Air Command was outdated intelligence.[3] The U.S. was relying solely

---

1 Geoffrey Perret, *Eisenhower* (Holbrook: Adams Media Corporation, 1999), 597.
2 John Lewis Gaddis, *Strategies of Containment: A Critical Appraisal of American National Security Policy during the Cold War* (Oxford: Oxford Press, 2005), 173.
3 Perret, *Eisenhower*, 597.

on intelligence taken from Germany during World War II to determine essential target locations in the event of a nuclear war.[4]

In order to update the knowledge of the United States intelligence about potential Soviet targets, the head of Strategic Air Command, Curtis LeMay, asked for a new avenue for intelligence gathering.[5] Since the Soviet had rejected the Open Skies proposal, the U.S. would have to rely on espionage to crack Soviet secrecy.[6] LeMay asked for a new spy plane to be created for the collecting of intelligence against the Soviet Union.[7] LeMay believed in an approach to war that made the ability to hit the enemy with every option available essential.[8] In order to hit the enemy with that type of force, an accurate reading of what the enemy had in its possession was vital.

While the U.S. intelligence community was awaiting the creation of the new plane, they relied on balloons to float into communist territory for collecting the much needed information. The balloons were met with only limited success.[9] A break-through occurred in 1954 when a committee recommended building a spy plane that would be able to safely fly over Soviet airspace and

---

4   Ibid.
5   Ibid.
6   Ibid., 583.
7   Ibid., 597.
8   Thomas, *Ike's Bluff*, 271.
9   Perret, *Eisenhower*, 597.

collect information to prepare the United States for potential war.[10] In December of 1954, President Eisenhower approved the project that would become the U-2 spy plane.[11]

Eisenhower had fallen in love with the idea of espionage and covert operations against Cold War threats early in his administration. The United States successfully toppled regimes deemed hostile to the long-term peace and safety of the United States. The CIA helped overthrow and replace communist-leaning governments and leaders in Iran and later in Guatemala.[12] Eisenhower and the CIA signed off on countless other operations throughout the world to strengthen America's hand in the struggle against communism.[13] With the history of espionage and secret operations against potentially threatening nations in mind, the development of the U-2 was a natural step for the Eisenhower administration.

The U-2 flights would enable the United States to gain a wealth of knowledge of Soviet military capabilities. However, a 1960 flight would temporarily change the face of the Cold War and give the United States a major gaffe in Cold War diplomacy. Eisenhower had given his approval for one last U-2 flight over Soviet territory in the spring of 1960. He also ordered the flight

---

10 Ibid,
11 Ibid., 580.
12 William I. Hitchcock, *The Age of Eisenhower: America and the World in the 1950s* (New York: Simon and Schuster, 2018), 148
13 Ibid.

scrapped if it was unable to occur on, or before, May 1, 1960.[14] The flight was delayed by weather until the deadline date.

The pilot chosen to make the U-2 flight was one of the most experienced pilots available for the mission, Francis Gary Powers.[15] This mission was important and potentially dangerous with President Eisenhower set to meet with Soviet leader Nikita Khrushchev in Paris on May 16, 1960.[16] There was little cause for alarm since this was mostly a routine flight being a made by an experienced pilot. Powers had flown the U-2 before on surveillance missions that ended with success for the United States.[17]

The routine nature of the flight began to change when Powers failed to reach his destination at the expected time and the Soviets stopped tracking his plane.[18] The United States still had little reason to panic since the likelihood of Powers and the plane surviving a potential crash were minimal.[19] There was little chance of the plane or the pilot falling into Soviet hands. This would prove to be a disastrous miscalculation by the United States government.

---

14 Jim Newton, *Eisenhower: The White House Years* (New York: First Anchor Books, 2012), 313.
15 Ibid.
16 Ibid.
17 Robert H. Ferrell, ed., *The Eisenhower Diaries*, (New York: W.W. Norton and Company, 19810, 330-331.
18 Newton, *Eisenhower*, 313.
19 Ibid.

The United States government however, almost immediately began to cover its tracks in the wake of the missing U-2. The problem for the U.S. was the fact that concealing the espionage would only be possible if the plane and the pilot were destroyed and killed. There was little room for concern considering how unlikely survival was for the pilot. There was also no reason to believe a cover-up would not work in this situation given what the U.S. government knew about the plane and the altitude at which it usually flew.

As news of the missing plane and pilot hit the United States, the government began releasing official statements to provide cover for the operation. On May 2, 1960, the government circulated the top-secret cover plan among the necessary agencies. Acknowledging the probable death of the pilot and stating the government was withholding his name until his family could be notified, the document read:

> Following is cover plan to be implemented immediately: 'U-2 aircraft was on weather mission originating Adana, Turkey. Purpose was study of clear air turbulence.
>
> During flight in Southeast Turkey, pilot reported he had oxygen difficulties. This last word heard at 0700Z over emergency frequency. U-2

aircraft did not land Adana as planned and it can only be assumed is now down. A search effort is under way in Lake Van area'

FYI normal procedures for search for aircraft will be initiated by Adana Base Commander and initial press release will be from Adana.[20]

Hoping that the world would buy the explanation and the issue would quickly pass, the Eisenhower administration continued to prepare for another meeting with Khrushchev. The National Aeronautics and Space Administration (NASA) released their own press release on May 5, 1960 to corroborate the missing weather plan message. Stating that the U-2 plane had been "in use since 1956 in a continuing program to study gust-meteorological conditions found at high altitudes,"[21] NASA helped continue to give cover to the actual events surrounding the missing U-2.

The NASA release also went on to state the missing status of the pilot. Giving specific details about the location, departure time, and alleged mission, the release indicated nothing more than

---

20 Cover Plan to Be Used for Downed U-2 Flight (the U.S. Did Not Know That the Soviets Had the Captured U.S. Pilot), May 2, 1960 (PDF) [Office of the Staff Secretary, Subject Series, Alphabetical Subseries, Box 15, Intelligence 14; NAID Number 594364] www.dwightdeisenhower.com

21 National Aeronautics and Space Administration Press Release Concerning Missing U-2 Airplane, May 5, 1960 (PDF) [Christian Herter Papers, Box 20, U-2 (1); NAID Number 12009392]

a routine weather mission gone wrong. Explaining why the pilot may have ended up inside territory unintended by the original flight path, NASA claimed the pilot had taken off from Turkey, but he was unable to continue on his stated course due to a lack of oxygen inside his plane.[22]

To further explain the path of the pilot, the NASA release claimed, "…his flight plan called for him to make a left turn at the Lake Van Beacon. His last report indicated he was attempting to receive that Beacon. It is believed he probably was on a northeasterly course, but there was no further word."[23]

As it became apparent that Khrushchev would double-down on his claim that the Soviet Union had shot down what they believed to be a U.S. spy plane, the United States State Department issued a May 6th press release restating the weather plan cover story. Directly referencing the Soviet claim of U.S. spy plane entering Soviet air space, the release read, "As already announced on May3, a United States National Aeronautical and Space Agency unarmed weather research plane based at Adana, Turkey, and piloted by a civilian American has been missing since May1. The name of the American civilian pilot is Francis

---

22 Ibid.
23 Ibid.

Gary Powers."[24] The State Department also asked the Soviet Union to release information about the fate of the pilot who had been reported missing.[25]

Within the next few days, it became obvious the United States was caught red-handed in an act of espionage. The Soviet Union produced evidence of the survival of Powers providing indisputable evidence of U.S. spying on Soviet installations. It is understandable that the U.S. government did not expect Francis Gary Powers to have survived the crash due to the high altitude capabilities of the U-2 in addition to the fact that he had been given a suicide needle to ensure he would not fall into enemy hands. Instead of going down with his plane or using the needle, Powers had followed the very human instinct of survival. He ejected from the plane, deployed his parachute, and attempted to survive after being shot down. A Washington Post article from May 12, 1960 indicated that Powers was not expected to use the suicide needle unless being tortured by the Soviets.[26] This allowed him to fall into the hands of the Soviet government and become a "prisoner of war" in

---

24 State Department Press Release Number 249 Concerning U-2 Incident, May 6, 1960 (PDF) [Christian Herter Papers, Box 20, U-2 (1); NAID Number 12009394]

25 Ibid.

26 Dwightdeisenhower.com. (2018). [online] Available at: https://www.dwightdeisenhower.com/DocumentCenter/View/2834/Washington-Post-Article-US-Heard-Russians-Chasing-U-2-May-12-1960-PDF?bidId= [Accessed 4 Jul. 2018].

a war that did not technically exist. The Cold War often created such complexities in international relations.

Finally, on May 9, 1960, the United States State Department issued another press release. This time, the State Department directly blamed the Soviet Union for the entire U-2 incident and did not shy away from the U.S. government's role in espionage against the Soviet Union. This press release stated the importance of aerial surveillance to the United States given the current world situation in 1960. The State Department now firmly placed the blame for the uneasiness felt on both sides directly at the feet of current, and former, Soviet leadership.[27]

The State Department was now willing and able to make the case against the Soviet Union for the communist being the guilty party in allowing the world to enter into an age when U-2 style spy planes were necessary by stating, "Ever since Marshal Stalin shifted the policy of the Soviet Union from a wartime cooperation to postwar conflict in 1946…the world has lived in a state of apprehension with respect to Soviet intentions."[28] The U.S. masterfully painted the Soviets as the post-World War II villains while painting itself with the bright colors of defender of the free world. Solidifying this role for the U.S., the press release

---

27 State Department Press Release Number 254 Concerning U-2 Incident, May 9, 1960 (PDF) [Christian Herter Papers, Box 20, U-2 (1); NAID Number 12009396)]
28 Ibid.

went on to read, "For many years, the United States in company with its allies has sought to lessen or even to eliminate this threat from the life of man,"[29] The State Department clearly argued that the Soviets could have avoided the entire U-2 incident if they had accepted President Eisenhower's "open skies" proposal. Open skies would have allowed both sides to keep a watchful eye on the nuclear buildup of the other nation. Transparency would have ruled the day making the U-2 and other spying techniques unnecessary.

President Eisenhower responded with his own press release on May 11, 1960 addressing the U-2 incident. The president resolutely stated the need for surveillance on the Soviet Union due to their actions and refusal to open their military facilities to the world for the sake of world peace. According to Eisenhower, the U-2 was necessary because, "The need for intelligence gathering activities… No one wants another Pearl Harbor. This means we must have knowledge of military forces and preparations around the world, especially those capable of massive surprise attack…Secrecy in the Soviet Union makes this essential. In most of the world no large-scale attack could be prepared in secret. But in the Soviet Union there is a fetish of secrecy and concealment."[30] President Dwight Eisenhower exposed the need to keep a watchful eye on

---

29 Ibid.
30 Statement by the President Regarding U-2 Incident, May 11, 1960 (PDF) [Christian Herter Papers, Box 20, U-2 (1); NAID Number 12009412

the Soviet Union by not only playing the role of commander-in-chief, but by assuming the role of the free world's lawyer in the court of the Cold War.

Reaction to the revelation of U.S. spying around the world seemed to fall along Cold War party lines. Almost all of the western world appreciated the imitative taken by the United States to watch the Soviet Union more closely. The Soviets used the incident to put the Paris summit in jeopardy announcing Khrushchev would only be allowed to meet with Eisenhower if he issued a public apology for sending the U-2 into Soviet airspace.[31] Eisenhower stood defiantly firm in his defense of the necessity of the U-2 flights. Western allies such as Charles de Gaulle supported Eisenhower during this tense moment of the Cold War telling Eisenhower, "whatever happens, we are with you."[32]

The Powers incident gave leverage to Khrushchev to claim innocence in the Cold War espionage game. He was able to viciously foam at the United States as a victim of the capitalistic nation's aggression. Eisenhower's reluctance to initially expose the downed plane as a spy craft had given some gamesmanship leverage to Khrushchev. Backing down however, was not in the character of Dwight David Eisenhower. After the situation

---

31   Thomas, *Ike's Bluff*, 380-381
32   Ibid.

reached a fevered pitched, he continued to plow on with his Cold War objectives as would be expected from the leader of the free world. Nevertheless, even with Eisenhower receiving support from his allies and continuing to stand up for the values of freedom, any potential breakthrough in an effort to create a lasting peace with the Soviet Union appeared unlikely during his time in office. This became a major source of lamenting for Eisenhower. He truly wanted to create a lasting peace with the Soviet Union before his time as president came to a close.

IV

The Election of 1960

With the U-2 incident and other Cold War episodes fresh in their minds, the American people were called upon to choose Eisenhower's successor to the presidency in 1960. The Cold War was one the primary focuses of most voters as the November election approached. Eisenhower's popularity remained strong in 1960, but fears were beginning to arise that he may have been overmatched at times by the Soviet Union. The trust placed in Eisenhower by the American people began to show some cracks as fears of Soviet Cold War supremacy began to take root. Some of his fellow-countrymen believed President Eisenhower had been asleep at the wheel and allowed the U.S. to fall to a strategic disadvantage in relation to Soviet missile capabilities. Historians have since proven these charges as utterly false in the aftermath of the Cold War.

The idea that the United States had fallen behind in the Cold War became a rallying point for the Democrat party in 1960. The

Democrat party nominated the young, handsome, Soviet-hating senator by the name of John F. Kennedy for president. Kennedy based the majority of his campaign on the accusation that Eisenhower's Republican administration had failed the American people. He repeatedly threw the accusation of America being on the wrong side of an alleged "missile gap" at the Eisenhower administration. Kennedy and his democrat allies painted Eisenhower as an aged grandfather who spent the past eight years playing golf and taking naps rather than effectively battling communists.

On the republican side of the election was Eisenhower's Vice-president Richard M. Nixon. Like Kennedy, Nixon was young for a presidential candidate. Also like his democrat opponent, Nixon was a famous champion of the anti-communists in the United States. Both men had entered congress around the same time, both moved up to the senate from the house of representatives around the same time, both were considered as vice-president candidates at an early age, and now they both had been tapped by their political parties to fight for the job of following Eisenhower into the White House.

The election of 1960 was going to illustrate a profound changing of the guard to a younger generation no matter who emerged victorious in the campaign. Both candidates had served in World War II and embodied the lessons of that era. Kennedy and Nixon came to view the world in terms of right and wrong, with the United States playing the role of righteous and the Soviet Union perfectly playing the villain. As members of the generation who defeated fascism and totalitarianism, both Kennedy and Nixon believed the world is more secure and stable when the United States is active and able to defeat nations who desire to force their will on others.

Richard Nixon entered the election of 1960 with a slight experience edge on Kennedy. With roughly the same amount of experience in terms of years in government, Nixon had the blessing to watch Eisenhower work on first-hand basis as vice-president. Even with the opposition pounding away with the "missile gap" attack, millions of Americans still viewed Eisenhower as a man they could trust with their lives and with the lives of their families. Being vice-president under such a trusted man would undoubtedly send many Americans to polling place to vote for Richard Nixon.

Unfortunately for Richard Nixon, his relationship with President Eisenhower was not as close as he may have wished. Eisenhower had flirted with the idea of removing Nixon from the presidential ticket during both elections. In 1952, before calling Nixon "his boy" and keeping him on the ticket with the success of the Checkers Speech,[1] Eisenhower first illustrated uneasiness with Nixon. Again, before the 1956 election, Eisenhower thought of replacing Nixon

---

[1] Ferrell, *Richard Nixon*, 177-197.

as vice-president and moving him into another position in the administration before again deciding to keep him. ²

During Eisenhower's many health scares as president, Nixon had performed remarkably well when faced with the commander-in-chief's inability to fulfill his duties. Nixon shined exceptionally bright during Eisenhower's heart attack that left the president unable to resume normal activities for a period of time. All of the positives of Nixon's association with Eisenhower was dealt a serious blow at a press conference during the election year in which Eisenhower stated he was unable to recall any policies Nixon had helped shape as vice-president when unexpectedly asked by a reporter to highlight Nixon's accomplishments.³ Without intending to do so, Eisenhower's inability to recall Nixon's contributions hurt Nixon's strongest pitch for being the next president. At a time when Americans feared nuclear weapons and the spread of communism, Eisenhower's answer made Nixon look like a nonfactor in his administration.

Nixon's campaign took another blow when he decided to face-off against Kennedy in the first televised presidential debates in American history. Believing he was the intellectually superior of

---

2 Ibid., 240-242
3 Pitney, Jack. "If You Give Me a Week, I Might Think of One." » Richard Nixon Foundation." Richard Nixon Foundation. September 08, 2016. Accessed November 08, 2018. https://www.nixonfoundation.org/2010/08/if-you-give-me-a-week-i-might-think-of-one/.

the two, Nixon accepted the idea to debate Kennedy on the new platform of television. The first debate took place on September 26, 1960[4] in front of an exceptionally large television audience. Still suffering from an illness related to an infection caused by bumping his knee shortly before the debate, Nixon appeared uncomfortable and flustered on television.[5] Kennedy on the other hand, appeared calm and collected throughout the debate. Kennedy emerged from the debate as exactly the kind of man many Americans wanted in the Oval Office to handle the tensions of the Cold War.

In all, there were four debates between John F. Kennedy and Richard Nixon in 1960. The last debate aired on October 21, 1960. The debates drew the largest television audience in the short history of the new media outlet. Even at its lowest time, the debate audiences still totaled 65,000,000.[6] Television now had the power to transform American politics.

The struggle for civil rights and how American would be perceived around the world arose yet again during the final stretch of the campaign. Emerging Civil Rights Movement leader Dr. Martin Luther King, Jr. had been imprisoned in Georgia for violating his parole from an expired driver's license.[7] Always a

---

4   White, *The Making of the President*, 279.
5   Ferrell, *Richard Nixon*, 283-287.
6   Theodore H. White, *The Making of the President, 1960* (New York: Harper Perennial, 2009), 283.
7   Steve Livingston, *Kennedy and King: The President, The Pastor, and the Battle over Civil Rights* (New York: Hachette Books, 2017), 71-72

delicate situation in the United States of that time, how to respond to a civil rights situation could make or break a candidate for national office. Especially with a man like King whose character would later be questioned in terms of the Cold War by the F.B.I.'s insistence that he had communist connections. Kennedy took the gamble and made a brief call to King's wife offering his support in the fight to see her husband released from prison. This action, courageous as it was during the Cold War and Civil Rights era, drew millions of African-Americans to Kennedy's side in the last days of the campaign. [8]

In one of the closest elections in American history, John F. Kennedy edged out Richard Nixon to become the thirty-fifth president of the United States by a little more than 100,000 votes.[9] With some discussions about the legality of the election results in some parts of the nation, a push for Nixon to challenge the results emerged. Nixon knew the Kennedy family had some tricks up their sleeves during the election, but the Nixon camp decided not to legally challenge the results in deference to national unity. After a discussion with President Eisenhower, Nixon realized the importance of accepting the results, and accepting the bitterly close defeat. Everything at that time played out in terms of the Cold War. Nixon graciously accepted the questionable results to

---

8   Ibid., 86-103.
9   White, *The Making of the President*, 385

deny the Soviet Union the opportunity to drag democracy through the mud on an international stage.

With the election of 1960 over, America was about to turn the page in its history once again. The youngest man ever elected was heading to the White House to replace the oldest president to have ever occupied the White House at that time. The Cold War was still raging. The tension between the United States and the Soviet Union was already high, but it was about to reach new and more dangerous heights. Amid all of this turmoil, Eisenhower would beautifully rise to the challenge of the peaceful transition of power and pave the way for his successor, John F. Kennedy.

V

Transition and Eisenhower's Farewell: The Calendar changes to 1961

Dwight Eisenhower's last act as president of the United States was perhaps his best moment as the leader of the American people. Although he was stung by the loss of Richard Nixon in the 1960 election, he was determined to see a smooth transition of power from his administration to the incoming Kennedy administration. This was a transition of power in one of the most hostile atmospheres imaginable. The U-2 blunder, trouble between China and Taiwan, the increasingly uneasy situation in Southeast Asia, and the rise of Fidel Castro as a communist ally in Cuba all hung over Washington, D.C. in the last days of the Eisenhower presidency. Eisenhower did not shrink from these challenges and wanted to ensure the new president was aware of just how volatile the world really was, and ensure Kennedy was as prepared as possible before Eisenhower handed him the reins of government.[1]

President-elect John F. Kennedy arrived at the White House on December 6, 1960 to begin the transition process.[2] Eisenhower showed the type of leadership Americans had come to admire in his meeting with Kennedy. During the campaign, Kennedy realized he was running against Eisenhower as much, if not at times more, than against Nixon. Kennedy was relentless in his attacks on Eisenhower's leadership, arguing the U.S. was falling behind in the Cold War due to Eisenhower being an ineffective steward of the executive branch. Eisenhower put that all behind him and worked hard to ensure a smooth transition. Kennedy left the December 6, 1960 meeting with Eisenhower with a new appreciation for what he had brought to the nation as president during the 1950s.[3]

On January 17, 1961, Dwight Eisenhower bid the American people farewell. The president wanted his goodbye to be reminiscent of George Washington's Farewell Address. This meant Eisenhower planned to give a nonpartisan speech with advice that only a man with his stature could give. He had worked in the service of the American people his entire adult life. From West Point, to World

---

1   Hitchcock, *The Age of Eisenhower*, 497-503.
2   Ibid., 497
3   Ibid., 499-500.

War II, to the White House, he had faithfully served his nation and wanted to give a lasting farewell.[4]

In his speech from the White House, President Eisenhower spoke to the American people about what the role of government should be in a Cold War footing. Interestingly for a military man, arguably the most famous passage of the speech warned about "the military industrial complex" in American society. The United States was on a permanent war footing with no end in sight.[5] Eisenhower hope to answer the complex question about what danger this may pose to a republic stating, "Until the latest of our world conflicts, the United States had no armaments industry. American makers of plowshares could, with time and as required, make swords as well. But now we can no longer risk emergency improvisation of national defense; we have been compelled to create a permanent armaments industry of vast proportions… The prospect of domination of the nation's scholars by Federal employment, project allocations, and the power of money is ever present-and is gravely to be regarded."[6]

Arguably, no one realized the importance of a strong military more than Dwight Eisenhower. He had presided over the massive invasion of Europe and the destruction of Hitler's Germany. As

---

4 Ibid., 507-508.
5 Ibid.
6 Brett Baier and Catherine Whitney, *Three Days in January: Dwight Eisenhower's Final Mission* (New York: William Morrow, 2017), 206-207

president, he had seen military advances that made his World War II army obsolete in almost every way. He also knew that as long as the United States and the Soviet Union was locked in the Cold War that the military would become increasingly powerful and wield enormous influence in the decision making process of the federal government. Eisenhower saw himself as the elder statesman of the country and felt it was his duty to warn his fellow Americans about losing themselves in the Cold War. He feared that in an attempt to be prepared for the dangers that could appear at any moment, the United States would inadvertently turn its back on the principles of freedom that had allowed the nation to rise to the highest levels of worldwide admiration. He conveyed this message to the American people during his televised farewell address as his presidency came to a close.

Eisenhower worked diligently to continue to be an effective leader during his final days as president. He was mindful to ensure Kennedy had as much information as necessary to be a success president on day one of his administration. This was evident during their last meeting on January 19, 1960 that occurred two days after his farewell address. Not only were the outgoing and incoming president at this final meeting, but the main members of the Kennedy team met with the high ranking members of the Eisenhower cabinet.[7] The men who would take over the U.S. government the next day received an

---

[7] Ibid., 238.

in-depth lesson about the dangers of the Cold War world from the seasoned veterans of the Eisenhower team.

The discussion touched on a number of hot spots around the world where communism seemed to be poised to make another attempt to enlarge its territory. One of the main focal points of the meeting was the increasingly alarming issue in Cuba. Fidel Castro had only been in power since 1959 when he overthrew the pro-American Cuban dictator Fulgencio Batista, but he was becoming a real problem for the United States.[8] No one in either administration was comfortable with the idea of having Castro so close to American shores.

Behind the scenes, the C.I.A. had hatched a plan to dispose of Castro. It was in the works when Eisenhower was still president but he ran out of time in office before he could decide if it should be implemented. Now, the plan would be passed on to Kennedy. Castro was becoming a close friend and ally to the Soviet Union and the C.I.A. believed they could successfully remove him from power. The plan called for C.I.A. trained Cuban exiles to invade Cuba and topple the Cuban leader.[9] The decision to implement the plan or not, now belonged to Kennedy.

As Eisenhower prepared to leave the White House, he was aware of his accomplishments. Even with the stinging criticism

---

8   Ibid., 239.
9   Ibid., 241.

from Democrats during the campaign, he remained very popular among the American people. It would take history a few decades to realize the success of Dwight Eisenhower and properly appreciate his leadership. Eisenhower was the man who stood up to the Soviet Union, modernized the military, ended the Korean War, kept American troops out of the jungles of Vietnam, protected our allies, pulled the world back from seemingly unstoppable nuclear annihilation, and was willing to make the tough decisions when needed. With the retrospect of history, Dwight D. Eisenhower was the right man, at the right time, to be president of the United States.

Part IV

Conclusion

JFK and Beyond

"...pay any price, bear any burden, meet any hardship, support any friend, oppose any foe to assure the survival and the success of liberty."
- President John F. Kennedy, 1961

On a cold, bright January day in 1961, the United States of America turned a corner. The nation welcomed its new president and signaled the beginning of something new. Men who had recently led armies of millions, or the nation as a whole, during World War II were now replaced with decades of presidents who had served in the lower levels of the military during that great conflict. It also became painfully clear that conventional wars were a thing of the past no matter how the new president's "flexible response" failed to realize it. This was a new America and a new world. The only real constant was the seemingly perpetual enemy of communism.

Standing before the snow covered capital that day, President John F. Kennedy delivered one of the most praised inaugural addresses in American history. His entire speech spoke to the role of the United States in the Cold War. He warned the nation's enemies, reassured the nation's allies, and raised the rhetoric of the Cold War promising to "pay any price, bear any burden, meet any hardship, support any friend, oppose any foe to assure the survival and success of liberty."[1] In many ways this speech was very different from the one President Eisenhower had delivered just a few days prior, but Kennedy was making it clear that "the torch has been passed to a new generation of the Americans."[2]

Kennedy's approach to the Cold War would play a role in bringing the world to the brink of annihilation. He would emerge from his time in office as a champion of the west and hardnosed foe of communism. During his time in office, Kennedy approved an ill-fated invasion of Cuba, met with an overbearing Nikita Khrushchev, watched the Berlin Wall go up, increase American involvement in Vietnam, stayed true to the belief in stopping the spread of communism, and ultimately be praised for saving

---

1   John Gabriel Hunt, ed., *The Inaugural Address of the Presidents: From George Washington to George W. Bush* (New York: Gramercy Books, 2005), 428.
2   Ibid.

civilization with restraint and celebrated leadership during the Cuban Missile Crisis.

There was no doubt that Kennedy was a Cold Warrior. He had built that reputation in the Senate as firm anti-communist leader. Kennedy also solidified that persona during the election of 1960 by perpetuating the missile gap myth. He came into office with an exuberant approach to stopping communism around the globe even if that meant not following in the footsteps of Eisenhower's strong but cautious approach.

President Eisenhower and President Truman did not fade away after their time in office expired. Eisenhower retreated to his Gettysburg farm where his expertise was often called upon by those who followed him into the White House. Perhaps, no president benefited more from Eisenhower genius than Kennedy in the days following the disastrous Bay of Pigs invasion. Kennedy met with the former president in the aftermath of the invasion and treated Eisenhower as an almost father figure on international affairs.

Eisenhower was called upon again by President Kennedy in the early days of the Cuban Missile Crisis in 1962. If only a brief conversation, Kennedy called Eisenhower to alert him of the situation and feel out how he would have responded to the situation. While no longer president, Eisenhower's leadership was still sought by those who followed him into government. No one had the credentials of Dwight Eisenhower.

The years to come would see Eisenhower's approach to the Cold War vindicated, Truman's rise to the ranks of America's best presidents, Kennedy receiving legend status, Nixon orchestrating the greatest political comeback and then tragedy in American history, and eventually victory over the Soviet Union in the Cold War. All the success that would come later in the waning days of the Cold War was built upon those first fifteen years…those Fifteen Years of Fear.

THE END

Appendixes

Appendix A

The Truman Doctrine Speech

President Harry S. Truman
March 12, 1947

The gravity of the situation which confronts the world today necessitates my appearance before a joint session of the Congress. The foreign policy and the national security of this country are involved.

One aspect of the present situation, which I wish to present to you at this time for your consideration and decision, concerns Greece and Turkey.

The United States has received from the Greek Government an urgent appeal for financial and economic assistance. Preliminary reports from the American Economic Mission now in Greece and reports from the American Ambassador in Greece corroborate the statement of the Greek Government that assistance is imperative if Greece is to survive as a free nation.

I do not believe that the American people and the Congress wish to turn a deaf ear to the appeal of the Greek Government.

Greece is not a rich country. Lack of sufficient natural resources has always forced the Greek people to work hard to make both ends meet. Since 1940, this industrious and peace-loving country has suffered invasion, four years of cruel enemy occupation, and bitter internal strife.

When forces of liberation entered Greece they found that the retreating Germans had destroyed virtually all the railways, roads, port facilities, communications and merchant marine. More than a thousand villages had been burned. Eighty-five per cent of the children were tubercular. Livestock, poultry and draft animals had almost disappeared. Inflation had wiped out practically all savings.

As a result of these tragic conditions, a military minority, exploiting human want and misery, was able to create political chaos which, until now, has made economic recovery impossible.

Greece is today without funds to finance the importation of those goods which are essential to bare subsistence. Under these circumstances the people of Greece cannot make progress in solving their problems of reconstruction. Greece is in desperate need of financial and economic assistance to enable it to resume purchases of food, clothing, fuel and seeds. These are indispensable for the subsistence of its people and are obtainable only from abroad. Greece must have help to import the goods necessary to restore internal order and security so essential for economic and political recovery.

The Greek Government has also asked for the assistance of experienced American administrators, economists and technicians to insure that the financial and other aid given to Greece shall be used effectively in creating a stable and self-sustaining economy and in improving its public administration.

The very existence of the Greek state is today threatened by the terrorist activities of several thousand armed men, led by Communists, who defy the Government's authority at a number of points, particularly along the northern boundaries. A commission appointed by the United Nations Security Council is at present investigating disturbed conditions in northern Greece and alleged border violations along the frontier between Greece on the one hand and Albania, Bulgaria and Yugoslavia on the other.

Meanwhile, the Greek Government is unable to cope with the situation. The Greek Army is small and poorly equipped. It needs supplies and equipment if it is to restore the authority of the Government throughout Greek territory.

Greece must have assistance if it is to become a self-supporting and self-respecting democracy.

The United States must supply that assistance. We have already extended to Greece certain types of relief and economic aid but these are inadequate. There is no other country to which democratic Greece can turn.

No other nation is willing and able to provide the necessary support for a democratic Greek Government.

The British Government, which has been helping Greece, can give no further financial or economic aid after March. Great Britain finds itself under the necessity of reducing or liquidating its commitments in several parts of the world, including Greece.

We have considered how the United Nations might assist in this crisis. But the situation is an urgent one requiring immediate action, and the United Nations and its related organizations are not in a position to extend help of the kind that is required.

It is important to note that the Greek Government has asked for our aid in utilizing effectively the financial and other assistance we may give to Greece, and in improving public administration. It is of the utmost importance that we supervise the use of any funds made available to Greece, in such a manner that each dollar spent will count toward making Greece self-supporting, and will help to build an economy in which a healthy democracy can flourish.

No government is perfect. One of the chief virtues of a democracy, however, is that its defects are always visible and under democratic processes can be pointed out and corrected. The Government of Greece is not perfect. Nevertheless it represents 85 per cent of the members of the Greek parliament who were chosen in an election last year. Foreign observers, including 692 Americans, considered this election to be a fair expression of the views of the Greek people.

The Greek Government has been operating in an atmosphere of chaos and extremism. It has made mistakes. The extension of aid by this country does not mean that the United States condones everything that the Greek Government has done or will do. We have condemned in the past, and we condemn now, extremist measures of the Right or the Left. We have in the past advised tolerance, and we advise tolerance now.

Greece's neighbor, Turkey, also deserves our attention.

The future of Turkey as an independent and economically sound State is clearly no less important to the freedom-loving peoples of the world than the future of Greece. The circumstances in which Turkey finds itself today are considerably different from those of Greece. Turkey has been spared the disasters that have beset Greece. And during the war, the United States and Great Britain furnished Turkey with material aid.

Nevertheless, Turkey now needs our support.

Since the war Turkey has sought financial assistance from Great Britain and the United States for the purpose of effecting that modernization necessary for the maintenance of its national integrity.

That integrity is essential to the preservation of order in the Middle East.

The British Government has informed us that, owing to its own difficulties, it can no longer extend financial or economic aid to Turkey.

As in the case of Greece, if Turkey is to have the assistance it needs, the United States must supply it. We are the only country able to provide that help.

I am fully aware of the broad implications involved if the United States extends assistance to Greece and Turkey, and I shall discuss these implications with you at this time.

One of the primary objectives of the foreign policy of the United States is the creation of conditions in which we and other nations will be able to work out a way of life free from coercion. This was a fundamental issue in the war with Germany and Japan.

Our victory was won over countries which sought to impose their will, and their way of life, upon other nations.

To ensure the peaceful development of nations, free from coercion, the United States has taken a leading part in establishing the United Nations. The United Nations is designed to make possible lasting freedom and independence for all its members. We shall not realize our objectives, however, unless we are willing to help free people to maintain their free institutions and their national integrity against aggressive movements that seek to impose upon them totalitarian regimes.

This is no more than a frank recognition that totalitarian regimes imposed on free peoples, by direct or indirect aggression, undermine the foundations of international peace and hence the security of the United States.

The peoples of a number of countries of the world have recently had totalitarian regimes forced upon them against their will. The Government of the United States has made frequent protests against coercion and intimidation in violation of the Yalta agreement, in Poland, Rumania, and Bulgaria. I must also state that in a number of other countries there have been similar developments.

At the present moment in world history nearly every nation must choose between alternative ways of life. The choice is too often not a free one.

One way of life is based upon the will of the majority, and is distinguished by free institutions, representative government, free elections, guarantees of individual liberty, freedom of speech and religion, and freedom from political oppression.

The second way of life is based upon the will of a minority forcibly imposed upon the majority. It relies upon terror and oppression, a controlled press and radio, fixed elections, and the suppression of personal freedoms.

I believe that it must be the policy of the United States to support free peoples who are resisting attempted subjugation by armed minorities or by outside pressures. I believe that we must assist free peoples to work out their own destinies in their own way. I believe that our help should be primarily through economic and financial aid which is essential to economic stability and orderly political processes.

The world is not static, and the status quo is not sacred. But we cannot allow changes in the status quo in violation of the Charter of the United Nations by such methods as coercion, or by such subterfuges as political infiltration. In helping free and independent nations to maintain their freedom, the United States will be giving effect to the principles of the Charter of the United Nations.

It is necessary only to glance at a map to realize that the survival and integrity of the Greek nation are of grave importance in a much wider situation. If Greece should fall under the control of an armed minority, the effect upon its neighbor, Turkey, would be immediate and serious. Confusion and disorder might well spread throughout the entire Middle East.

Moreover, the disappearance of Greece as an independent State would have a profound effect upon those countries in Europe whose peoples are struggling against great difficulties to maintain their freedoms and their independence while they repair the damages of war. It would be an unspeakable tragedy if these countries, which have struggled so long against overwhelming odds, should lose that victory for which they sacrificed so much. Collapse of free institutions and loss of independence would be disastrous not only for them but for the world.

Discouragement and possibly failure would quickly be the lot of neighboring peoples striving to maintain their freedom and independence.

Should we fail to aid Greece and Turkey in this fateful hour, the effect will be far-reaching to the West as well as to the East. We must take immediate and resolute action.

I therefore ask the Congress to provide authority for assistance to Greece and Turkey in the amount of $400,000,000 for the period ending June 30, 1948. In requesting these funds, 1 have taken into consideration the maximum amount of relief assistance which would be furnished to Greece out of the $350,000,000 which I recently requested that the Congress authorize for the prevention of starvation and suffering in countries devastated by the war.

In addition to funds, I ask the Congress to authorize the detail of American civilian and military personnel to Greece and Turkey, at the request of those countries, to assist in the tasks of reconstruction, and for the purpose of supervising the use of such financial and material assistance as may be furnished. I recommend that authority also be provided for the instruction and training of selected Greek and Turkish personnel.

Finally, I ask that the Congress provide authority which will permit the speediest and most effective use, in terms of needed commodities, supplies and equipment, of such funds as may be authorized.

If further funds, or further authority, should be needed for purposes indicated in this message, I shall not hesitate to bring the situation before the Congress. On this subject the executive and legislative branches of the Government must work together.

This is a serious course upon which we embark. I would not recommend it except that the alternative is much more serious.

The United States contributed $341,000,000,000 toward winning World War II. This is an investment in world freedom and world peace. The assistance that I am recommending for

Greece and Turkey amounts to little more than one-tenth of one per cent of this investment. It is only common sense that we should safeguard this investment and make sure that it was not in vain.

The seeds of totalitarian regimes are nurtured by misery and want. They spread and grow in the evil soil of poverty and strife. They reach their full growth when the hope of a people for a better life has died. We must keep that hope alive.

The free peoples of the world look to us for support in maintaining their freedoms. If we falter in our leadership, we may endanger the peace of the world and we shall surely endanger the welfare of our own nation.

Great responsibilities have been placed upon us by the swift movement of events. I am confident that the Congress will face these responsibilities squarely.

Source: Truman, Harry S. "The Truman Doctrine." Teaching American History. Accessed May 30, 2018. http://teachingamericanhistory.org/library/document/the-truman-doctrine/.

Appendix B

The Marshall Plan Speech

Secretary of State George C. Marshall
June 5, 1947

Mr. President, Dr. Conant, members of the board of overseers, ladies and gentlemen, I'm profoundly grateful and touched by the distinction and honor and great compliment accorded me by the authorities of Harvard this morning. I'm overwhelmed, as a matter of fact, and I'm rather fearful of my inability to maintain such a high rating as you've been generous enough to accord to me. In these historic and lovely surroundings, this perfect day, and this very wonderful assembly, it is a tremendously impressive thing to an individual in my position.

I need not tell you gentlemen that the world situation is very serious. That must be apparent to all intelligent people. I think one difficulty is that the problem is one of such enormous complexity that the very mass of facts presented to the public by press and radio make it exceedingly difficult for the man in the street to reach a clear appraisement of the situation. Furthermore, the people of this country are distant from the troubled areas of the earth and it is hard for them to comprehend the plight and consequent reactions of the long-suffering peoples, and the effect of those reactions on their governments in connection with our efforts to promote peace in the world.

In considering the requirements for the rehabilitation of Europe the physical loss of life, the visible destruction of cities, factories, mines and railroads was correctly estimated, but it has become obvious during recent months that this visible destruction was probably less serious than the dislocation of the entire fabric of European economy. For the past ten years conditions have been highly abnormal. The feverish preparation for war and the more feverish maintenance of the war effort engulfed all aspects of national economies. Machinery has fallen into disrepair or is entirely obsolete. Under the arbitrary and destructive Nazi rule, virtually every possible enterprise was geared into the German war machine. Long-standing commercial ties, private institutions, banks, insurance companies and shipping companies disappeared, through loss of capital, absorption through nationalization or by simple destruction. In many countries, confidence in the local currency has been severely shaken. The breakdown of the business structure of Europe during the war was complete. Recovery has been seriously retarded by the fact that two years after the close of hostilities a peace settlement with Germany and Austria has not been agreed upon. But even given a more prompt solution of these difficult problems, the rehabilitation of the economic structure of Europe quite evidently will require a much longer time and greater effort than had been foreseen.

There is a phase of this matter which is both interesting and serious. The farmer has always produced the foodstuffs to exchange with the city dweller for the other necessities of life. This division of labor is the basis of modern civilization. At the present time it is threatened with breakdown. The town and city industries are not producing adequate goods to exchange with the food-producing farmer. Raw materials and fuel are in short supply. Machinery is lacking or worn out. The farmer of the peasant cannot find the goods for sale which he desires to purchase. So the sale of his farm produce for money which he cannot use seems to him an unprofitable transaction. He, therefore, has withdrawn many fields from crop cultivation and is using them for grazing. He feeds more grain to stock and finds for himself and his family an ample supply of food, however short he may be on clothing and the other ordinary gadgets of civilization. Meanwhile people in the cities are short of food and fuel. So the governments are forced to use their foreign money and credits to procure these necessities abroad. This process exhausts funds which are urgently needed for reconstruction. This a very serious situation is rapidly developing which bodes no good for the world. The modern system of the division of labor upon which the exchange of products is based is in danger of breaking down.

The truth of the matter is that Europe's requirements for the next three or four years of foreign food and other essential products–principally from America–are so much greater than her present ability to pay that she must have substantial additional help, or face economic, social and political deterioration of a very grave character.

The remedy lies in breaking the vicious circle and restoring the confidence of the European people in the economic future of their own countries and of Europe as a whole. The manufacturer and the farmer throughout wide areas must be able and willing to exchange their products for currencies the continuing value of which is not open to question.

Aside from the demoralizing effect on the world at large and the possibilities of disturbances arising as a result of the desperation of the people concerned, the consequences to the economy of the United States should be apparent to all. It is logical that the United States should do whatever it is able to do to assist in the return of normal economic health in the world, without which there can be no political stability and no assured peace. Our policy is directed not against any country or doctrine but against hunger, poverty, desperation and chaos. Its purpose should be the revival of a working economy in the world so as to permit the emergence of political and social conditions in which free institutions can exist. Such assistance, I am convinced, must not be on a piece-meal basis as various crises develop. Any assistance that this Government may render in the future should provide a cure rather than a mere palliative. Any government that is willing to assist in the task of recovery will find full cooperation, I am sure, on the part of the United States Government. Any government which maneuvers to block the recovery of other countries cannot expect help from us. Furthermore, governments, political parties or groups which seek to perpetuate human misery in order to profit therefrom politically or otherwise will encounter the opposition of the United States.

It is already evident that, before the United States Government can proceed much further in its efforts to alleviate the situation and help start the European world on its way to recovery, there must be some agreement among the countries of Europe as to the requirements of the situation and the part those countries themselves will take in order to give proper effect to whatever action might be undertaken by this Government. It would be neither fitting nor efficacious for this Government to undertake to draw up unilaterally a program designed to place Europe on its feet economically. This is the business of the Europeans. The initiative,

I think, must come from Europe. The role of this country should consist of friendly aid in the drafting of a European program and of later support of such a program so far as it may be practical for us to do so. The program should be a joint one, agreed to by a number, if not all European nations.

An essential part of any successful action on the part of the United States is an understanding on the part of the people of America of the character of the problem and the remedies to be applied. Political passion and prejudice should have no part. With foresight, and a willingness on the part of our people to face up to the vast responsibility which history has clearly placed upon our country, the difficulties I have outlined can and will be overcome.

I am sorry that on occasion I have said something publicly in regard to our international situation; I've been forced by the necessities of the case to enter into rather technical discussions. But to my mind, it is of vast importance that our people reach some general understanding of what the complications really are, rather than react from a passion or a prejudice or an emotion of the moment. As I said more formally a moment ago, we are remote from the scene of these troubles. It is virtually impossible at this distance merely by reading, or listening, or even seeing photographs or motion pictures, to grasp at all the real significance of the situation. And yet the whole world of the future hangs on a proper judgment. It hangs, I think, to a large extent on the realization of the American people, of just what are the various dominant factors. What are the reactions of the people? What are the justifications of those reactions? What are the sufferings? What is needed? What can best be done? What must be done? Thank you very much.

Source: "The Marshall Plan Speech." George C Marshall. Accessed May 30, 2018. https://www.marshallfoundation.org/marshall/the-marshall-plan/marshall-plan-speech/.

Appendix C

Farewell Address

President Dwight D. Eisenhower
January 17, 1961

Good evening, my fellow Americans: First, I should like to express my gratitude to the radio and television networks for the opportunity they have given me over the years to bring reports and messages to our nation. My special thanks go to them for the opportunity of addressing you this evening.

Three days from now, after a half century of service of our country, I shall lay down the responsibilities of office as, in traditional and solemn ceremony; the authority of the Presidency is vested in my successor.

This evening I come to you with a message of leave-taking and farewell, and to share a few final thoughts with you, my countrymen.

Like every other citizen, I wish the new President, and all who will labor with him, Godspeed. I pray that the coming years will be blessed with peace and prosperity for all.

Our people expect their President and the Congress to find essential agreement on questions of great moment, the wise resolution of which will better shape the future of the nation.

My own relations with Congress, which began on a remote and tenuous basis when, long ago, a member of the Senate appointed me to West Point, have since ranged to the intimate during the war and immediate post-war period, and finally to the mutually interdependent during these past eight years.

In this final relationship, the Congress and the Administration have, on most vital issues, cooperated well, to serve the nation well rather than mere partisanship, and so have assured that the business of the nation should go forward. So my official relationship with Congress ends in a feeling on my part, of gratitude that we have been able to do so much together.

We now stand ten years past the midpoint of a century that has witnessed four major wars among great nations. Three of these involved our own country. Despite these holocausts America is today the strongest, the most influential and most productive nation in the world. Understandably proud of this pre-eminence, we yet realize that America's leadership and prestige depend, not merely upon our unmatched material progress, riches and military strength, but on how we use our power in the interests of world peace and human betterment.

Throughout America's adventure in free government, such basic purposes have been to keep the peace; to foster progress in human achievement, and to enhance liberty, dignity and integrity among peoples and among nations.

To strive for less would be unworthy of a free and religious people.

Any failure traceable to arrogance or our lack of comprehension or readiness to sacrifice would inflict upon us a grievous hurt, both at home and abroad.

Progress toward these noble goals is persistently threatened by the conflict now engulfing the world. It commands our whole attention, absorbs our very beings. We face a hostile ideology global in scope, atheistic in character, ruthless in purpose, and insidious in method. Unhappily the danger it poses promises to be of indefinite duration. To meet it successfully, there is called for, not so much the emotional and transitory sacrifices of crisis, but rather those which enable us to carry forward steadily, surely, and without complaint the burdens of a prolonged and complex struggle—with liberty the stake. Only thus shall we remain, despite every provocation, on our charted course toward permanent peace and human betterment.

Crises there will continue to be. In meeting them, whether foreign or domestic, great or small, there is a recurring temptation to feel that some spectacular and costly action could become the miraculous solution to all current difficulties. A huge increase in the newer elements of our defenses; development of unrealistic programs to cure very ill in agriculture; a dramatic expansion in basic and applied research—these and many other possibilities, each possibly promising in itself, may be suggested as the only way to the road we wish to travel.

But each proposal must be weighed in light of a broader consideration; the need to maintain balance in and among national programs—balance between the private and the public economy, balance between the cost and hoped for advantages—balance between the clearly necessary and the comfortably desirable; balance between our essential requirements as a nation and the duties imposed by the nation upon the individual; balance between the actions of the moment and the national welfare of the future. Good judgment seeks balance and progress; lack of it eventually finds imbalance and frustration.

The record of many decades stands as proof that our people and their Government have, in the main, understood these truths and have responded to them well in the face of threat and stress.

But threats, new in kind or degree, constantly arise.

Of these, I mention two only.

A vital element in keeping the peace is our military establishment. Our arms must be mighty, ready for instant action, so that no potential aggressor may be tempted to risk his own destruction.

Our military organization today bears little relation to that known by any of my predecessors in peacetime, or indeed by the fighting men of World War II or Korea.

Until the latest of our world conflicts, the United States had no armaments industry. American makers of plowshares could, with time and as required, make swords as well. But now we can no longer risk emergency improvisation of national defense; we have been compelled to create a permanent armaments industry of vast proportions. Added to this, three and a half million men and women are directly engaged in the defense establishment. We annually spend on military security more than the net income of all United States corporations.

This conjunction of an immense military establishment and a large arms industry is new in the American experience. The total influence—economic, political, even spiritual—is felt in every city, every Statehouse, every office of the Federal government. We recognize the imperative need for this development. Yet we must not fail to comprehend its grave implications. Our toil, resources and livelihood are all involved; so is the very structure of our society.

In the councils of government, we must guard against the acquisition of unwarranted influence, whether sought or unsought, by the military-industrial complex. The potential for the disastrous rise of misplaced power exists and will persist.

We must never let the weight of this combination endanger our liberties or democratic processes. We should take nothing for granted. Only an alert and knowledgeable citizenry can compel the proper meshing of the huge industrial and military machinery of defense with our peaceful methods and goals, so that security and liberty may prosper together.

Akin to, and largely responsible for the sweeping changes in our industrial-military posture, has been the technological revolution during recent decades.

In this revolution, research has become central, it also becomes more formalized, complex, and costly. A steadily increasing share is conducted for, by, or at the direction of, the Federal government.

Today, the solitary inventor, tinkering in his shop, has been overshadowed by task forces of scientists in laboratories and testing fields. In the same fashion, the free university, historically the fountainhead of free ideas and scientific discovery, has experienced a revolution in the conduct of research. Partly because of the huge costs involved, a government contract becomes virtually a substitute for intellectual curiosity. For every old blackboard there are now hundreds of new electronic computers.

The prospect of domination of the nation-s scholars by Federal employment, project allocations, and the power of money is ever present—and is gravely to be regarded.

Yet, in holding scientific research and discovery in respect, as we should, we must also be alert to the equal and opposite danger that public policy could itself become the captive of a scientific-technological elite.

It is the task of statesmanship to mold, to balance, and to integrate these and other forces, new and old, within the principles of our democratic system—ever aiming toward the supreme goals of our free society.

Another factor in maintaining balance involves the element of time. As we peer into society's future, we—you and I, and our government—must avoid the impulse to live only for today, plundering for, for our own ease and convenience, the precious resources of tomorrow. We cannot mortgage the material assets of our grandchildren without asking the loss also of their political and spiritual heritage. We want democracy to survive for all generations to come, not to become the insolvent phantom of tomorrow.

Down the long lane of the history yet to be written America knows that this world of ours, ever growing smaller, must avoid becoming a community of dreadful fear and hate, and be, instead, a proud confederation of mutual trust and respect.

Such a confederation must be one of equals. The weakest must come to the conference table with the same confidence as do we, protected as we are by our moral, economic, and military strength. That table, though scarred by many past frustrations, cannot be abandoned for the certain agony of the battlefield.

Disarmament, with mutual honor and confidence, is a continuing imperative. Together we must learn how to compose differences, not with arms, but with intellect and decent purpose. Because this need is so sharp and apparent I confess that I lay down my official responsibilities in this field with a definite sense of disappointment. As one who has witnessed the horror and the lingering sadness of war–as one who knows that another war could utterly destroy this civilization which has been so slowly and painfully built over thousands of years–I wish I could say tonight that a lasting peace is in sight.

Happily, I can say that war has been avoided. Steady progress toward our ultimate goal has been made. But, so much remains to be done. As a private citizen, I shall never cease to do what little I can to help the world advance along that road.

So–in this my last good night to you as your President–I thank you for the many opportunities you have given me for public service in war and peace. I trust that in that service you find some things worthy; as for the rest of it, I know you will find ways to improve performance in the future.

You and I—my fellow citizens—need to be strong in our faith that all nations, under God, will reach the goal of peace with justice. May we be ever unswerving in devotion to principle, confident but humble with power, diligent in pursuit of the Nations' great goals.

To all the peoples of the world, I once more give expression to America's prayerful and continuing aspiration:

We pray that peoples of all faiths, all races, all nations, may have their great human needs satisfied; that those now denied opportunity shall come to enjoy it to the full; that all who yearn for freedom may experience its spiritual blessings; that those who have freedom will understand, also, its heavy responsibilities; that all who are insensitive to the needs of others will learn charity; that the scourges of poverty, disease and ignorance will be made to disappear from the earth, and that, in the goodness of time, all peoples will come to live together in a peace guaranteed by the binding force of mutual respect and love.

Now, on Friday noon, I am to become a private citizen. I am proud to do so. I look forward to it.

Thank you, and, good night.

Source: Teachingamericanhistory.org. (2018). Farewell Address to the Nation | Teaching American History. [online] Available at: http://teachingamericanhistory.org/library/document/farewell-address-to-the-nation/ [Accessed 4 Jul. 2018].

Bibliography

After Hitler, Directed by David Korn-Brzoza. Produced by Fabienne Servan Schreiber and Luci Pastor. France Television, 2016.

Alexander, Bevin. *MacArthur's War: The Flawed Genius who challenged the American Political System*. New York: Berkeley Publishing Group, 2013.

Ambrose, Stephen E. *Eisenhower: Soldier and President*. New York: Simon and Schuster Paperbacks, 1990.

Ambrose, Stephen E. *The Supreme Commander: The War Years of Dwight D. Eisenhower*. New York: Anchor Books, 2012.

Baier, Brett and Whitney, Catherine. *Three Days in January: Dwight Eisenhower's Final Mission*. New York: William Morrow, 2017.

Baime, A.J. *The Accidental President: Harry S. Truman and the Four Months that Changed the World. Boston:* Houghton Mifflin Harcourt, 2017.

Bennett, William J. America: *The Last Best Hope: Volume II: From a World at War to the Triumph of Freedom.* Nashville: Thomas Nelson.

Brands, H.W. *The General and the President: MacArthur and Truman at the Brink of Nuclear War.* New York: Doubleday, 2016.

Brands, H.W. *Traitor to his Class: The Privileged Life and Radical Presidency of Franklin Delano Roosevelt.* New York: Doubleday, 2008.

Brinkley, Alan. *John F. Kennedy.* New York: Times Books, Henry Holt and Company, LLC, 2012.

Brown, Archie. *The Rise and Fall of Communism.* New York: HarperCollins Publishers, 2009.

Burkett, Chris, ed. *50 Core American Documents: Required Reading for Students, Teachers, and Citizens. Ashland*: Ashbrook Press, 2013.

Chance for Peace Speech. Accessed July 10, 2017. https://www.eisenhower.archives.gov.

Cherny, Andrei. *The Candy Bombers: The Untold Story of the Berlin Airlift and America's Finest Hour.* New York: The Berkeley Publishing Group, 2008.

Cover Plan to Be Used for Downed U-2 Flight (the U.S. Did Not Know That the Soviets Had the Captured U.S. Pilot), May 2, 1960 (PDF) [Office of the Staff Secretary, Subject Series, Alphabetical Subseries, Box 15, Intelligence 14; NAID Number 594364] www.dwightdeisenhower.com.

Dallek, Robert. *Franklin D. Roosevelt: A Political Life.* New York: Viking, 2017.

Dallek, Robert. *An Unfinished Life: John F. Kennedy 1917-1963.* New York: Back Bay Books, 2013.

Dobbs, Michael. *Six Months in 1945: FDR, Stalin, Churchill, and Truman-From World War II to Cold War.* New York: Alfred A. Knopf, 2012.

Doran, Michael. *Ike's Gamble: America's Rise to Dominance in the Middle East.* New York: Free Press, 2016.

Duck and Cover (1951) Bert the Turtle. YouTube. Accessed March 13, 2018.

Dwightdeisenhower.com. (2018). [online] Available at: https://www.dwightdeisenhower.com/DocumentCenter/View/2834/Washington-Post-Article-US-Heard-Russians-Chasing-U-2-May-12-1960-PDF?bidId= [Accessed 4 Jul. 2018].

Ferrell, John A. *Richard Nixon: The Life*. New York: Doubleday, 2017.

Ferrell, Robert H., ed. *The Eisenhower Diaries*. New York: W.W. Norton and Company, 1981.

Ferrell, Robert H. *Harry S. Truman: A Life. Columbia*: University of Missouri Press, 1994.

Finder, Henry, ed. *The 50s: The Story of a Decade*. New York: Random House, 2015.

Foner, Eric. *Give Me Liberty: Volume 2, An American History 3rd Edition*. New York: W.W. Norton and Company, 2012.

Frank, Jeffrey. *Ike and Dick: A Portrait of a Strange Political Marriage*. New York: Simon and Schuster Paperbacks, 2013.

Gaddis, John Lewis. *George F. Kennan: An American Life*. New York: Penguin Books, 2011.

Gaddis, John Lewis. *Strategies of Containment: A Critical Appraisal of American National Security Policy during the Cold War.* Oxford: Oxford Press, 2005.

Gaddis, John Lewis. *The Cold War: A New History.* New York: Penguin Group, 2005.

Gaddis, John Lewis. *The United States and the Origins of the Cold War*: 1941-1945. New York: Columbia University Press, 2000.

Gaddis, John Lewis. *We Now Know: Rethinking Cold War History.* Oxford: Oxford University Press, 1997.

Gibbs, Nancy and Duffy, Michael. *The President's Club: Inside the World's Most Exclusive Fraternity.* New York: Simon and Schuster paperbacks, 2012.

Grayson, Benson Lee. *The American Image of China.* New York: Frederick Unger Publishing Co., 1979.

Hitchcock, William I. *The Age of Eisenhower: America and the World in the 1950s.* New York: Simon and Schuster, 2018.

Herman, Arthur. *Douglas MacArthur: American Warrior.* New York: Random House, 2016.

Hunt, John Gabriel, ed., *The Inaugural Address of the Presidents: From George Washington to George W. Bush*. New York: Gramercy Books, 2005.

Isaacson, Walter. *Einstein: His Life and Universe.* New York: Simon and Schuster Paperbacks, 2007.

Johnson, Paul. *Eisenhower: A Life*. New York: Penguin Books, 2014.

Keane, Jennifer, ed. *World War II Documents*. Ashland: Ashbrook Center, 2018.

Kiernan, Denise. *The Girls of Atomic City: The Untold Story of the Women who helped win World War II*. New York: Touchstone, 2013.

Korda, Michael. *Ike: An American Hero*. New York: Harper Collins, 2007.

Livingston, Steve. *Kennedy and King: The President, the Pastor, and the Battle over Civil Rights*. New York: Hachette Books, 2017.

Krugler, David, ed., *The Cold War: Core Documents*, Ashland: Ashbrook Press, 2018.

MacArthur, Douglas. *Reminisces*, New York: McGraw-Hill Book Company, 1964.

Meacham, Jon. *The Soul of America: The Battle for our Better Angels*, New York: Random House, 2018.

McCullough, *Truman*. New York: Simon and Schuster Paperbacks, 1992

NASA. Accessed March 24, 2018. https://history.nasa.gov/sputnik/.

Newton, Jim. *Eisenhower: The White House Years*. New York: First Anchor Books, 2012.

Nichols, David A. *Eisenhower 1956: The President's Year of Crisis, Suez and the Brink of War*. New York: Simon and Schuster Paperbacks, 2011.

Nichols, David A. *Ike and McCarthy: Dwight Eisenhower's Secret Campaign against Joseph McCarthy*. New York: Simon and Schuster, 2017.

Nixon, Richard. *RN: The Memoirs of Richard Nixon*. New York: Grossett & Dunlap, 1978.

Oliphant, Thomas and Wilkie, Curtis. *The Road to Camelot: Inside JFK's Five-Year Campaign*. New York: Simon and Schuster, 2017.

Perret, Geoffrey. *Eisenhower.* Holbrook: Adams Media Corporation, 1999.

Pitney, Jack. "If You Give Me a Week, I Might Think of One." » Richard Nixon Foundation." Richard Nixon Foundation. September 08, 2016. Accessed November 08, 2018. https://www.nixonfoundation.org/2010/08/if-you-give-me-a-week-i-might-think-of-one/.

Public Papers of the Presidents: Harry S. Truman 1945-1953. Special Message to the Congress on Greece and Turkey: The Truman Doctrine. Harry S. Truman Library and Museum. Accessed February 3, 2017.

Public Papers of the Presidents: Harry S. Truman 1945-1953. President's News Conference. Harry S. Truman Library and Museum. Accessed January 24, 2017.

National Aeronautics and Space Administration Press Release Concerning Missing U-2 Airplane, May 5, 1960 (PDF) [Christian Herter Papers, Box 20, U-2 (1); NAID Number 12009392].

National Security Act of 1947. Office of the Director of National Intelligence. Accessed February 10, 2017.

"Reaction to the Soviet Satellite - A Preliminary Evaluation." Dwight D. Eisenhower Presidential Library, Museum and Boyhood Home. Accessed March 24, 2018.

Smith, Jean Edward. *Eisenhower in War and Peace.* New York: Random House Trade Paperbacks, 2013.

Smith, Jean Edward. *FDR.* New York: Random House Paperbacks, 2007.

State Department Press Release Number 254 Concerning U-2 Incident, May 9, 1960 (PDF) [Christian Herter Papers, Box 20, U-2 (1); NAID Number 12009396)].

State Department Press Release Number 249 Concerning U-2 Incident, May 6, 1960 (PDF) [Christian Herter Papers, Box 20, U-2 (1); NAID Number 12009394].

Statement by the President Regarding U-2 Incident, May 11, 1960 (PDF) [Christian Herter Papers, Box 20, U-2 (1); NAID Number 12009412.

"Statement by the National Science Board in Response to Russian Satellite, October 1957." Dwight D. Eisenhower Presidential Library, Museum and Boyhood Home. Accessed

March 24, 2018. https://www.eisenhower.archives.gov/research/online_documents/sputnik.html.

Steil, Benn. *The Marshall Plan: Dawn of the Cold War.* New York: Simon and Schuster, 2018.

Teachingamericanhistory.org. (2018). Farewell Address to the Nation | Teaching American History. [online] Available at: http://teachingamericanhistory.org/library/document/farewell-address-to-the-nation/ [Accessed 4 Jul. 2018].

"The Sinews of Peace ('Iron Curtain Speech')." The International Churchill Society. April 13, 2017. Accessed March 23, 2018. https://www.winstonchurchill.org/resources/speeches/1946-1963-elder-statesman/the-sinews-of-peace/.

"The Marshall Plan Speech." George C Marshall. Accessed May 30, 2018. https://www.marshallfoundation.org/marshall/the-marshall-plan/marshall-plan-speech/.

Thomas, Evan. *Ike's Bluff: President Eisenhower's Secret Battle to Save the World.* New York: Little, Brown and Company, 2012.

Thomas, Evan. *Being Nixon: A Man Divided.* New York: Random House, 2015.

Truman, Harry S. "The Truman Doctrine." Teaching American History. Accessed May 30, 2018. http://teachingamericanhistory.org/library/document/the-truman-doctrine/.

Truman, Harry S., Truman, Margaret, ed. *Where the Buck Stops: The Personal and Private Writings of Harry S. Truman.* New York: Warner Books, Inc., 1989.

Truman, Margaret. *Harry S. Truman.* New York: William Morrow and Company, Inc., 1973.

U.S. Department of Defense, *Civil Defense Booklets: Volume 2, The Red Dog Nuclear Survival Series.* Red Dog Press, Inc., 2010.

Von Tunzelmann, Alex. *Blood and Sand: Suez, Hungary, and Eisenhower's Campaign for Peace.* New York: Harper Collins, 2016.

White, Theodore H. *The Making of the President*, 1960. New York: Harper Perennial, 2009.

Winik, Jay. *1944: The Year that Changed History.* New York: Simon and Schuster, 2015.

CPSIA information can be obtained
at www.ICGtesting.com
Printed in the USA
BVHW031241191218
535966BV00006B/70/P